BRAINHACKED

JENNIFER BEESTON

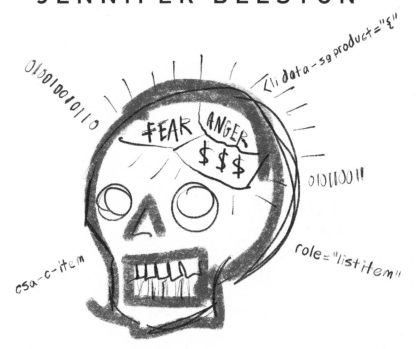

BRAINHACKED

HOW BIG TECH TRAINS YOUR BRAIN
TO SPEND—AND HOW TO FIGHT BACK

LIONCREST
PUBLISHING

BRAINHACKED
*How Big Tech Trains Your Brain to
Spend—And How to Fight Back*

FIRST EDITION

ISBN   978-1-5445-3521-0   *Hardcover*
       978-1-5445-3520-3   *Paperback*
       978-1-5445-3522-7   *Ebook*

CONTENTS

INTRODUCTION

Every day I took the same phone call, and heard a desperate person sobbing on the other end, asking the same helpless question: "Please, how can I save my house?"

It was 2007, and I'd just entered the mortgage industry as a fresh-faced newbie, with no clue that I was walking into the biggest real estate crash in US history. I felt like I was standing behind a plate-glass window four stories up, watching a child in the middle of the road about to get hit by a car. I could scream, I could pound on the glass, but there was nothing I could do to stop it.

Every time I heard that question, my heart broke a little bit more. I'd do what I could—refer them to a modification program, look at their financials, and see if there was another loan product that might help. Nothing helped. They were in too deep.

There was a consistent theme in all these calls—the homeowner had signed up for a complicated, exotic loan with no idea how it worked, and no ability to repay it when it came due. Most of the time, the loan officer who sold it to them didn't know how it worked either. Even if they'd asked all the right questions, they often didn't get a straight answer that they could understand.

I made it my mission to educate consumers so that they would never have to make that phone call, begging for help. I built my career on the principle that if I couldn't explain a mortgage product to a ten-year-old, I wouldn't recommend it to a client. The economy and the real estate market recovered, but I discovered a new problem.

Now I get calls from people who are afraid they will never be able to buy a home. They make plenty of money. They just don't understand where it's going. So I set out to write a book about mortgages and personal finance, because that's what I know and what I talk about every single day. Make a budget, stack cash, don't get scammed, and work the plan. Simple.

Then I looked around at all the solid financial advice that's already available. I realized that it isn't so simple anymore. Not in today's technologically advanced world. Most people already know the basics of money. They just don't understand how complex their own behavior has become. They have the best of intentions, but they feel like there's something overriding their good intentions. They don't know where their money is going because they are spending it without making any conscious decision to do so. Let me repeat that so it really sinks in: *they are spending their money without making any conscious decision to do so.*

How could that happen? Among my clients, it seemed to always come back to online shopping. Then I started looking at my own spending, and I saw the same pattern: purchases made impulsively, almost randomly. Purchases I didn't even remember making. I started researching all the ways that technology and digital marketing were persuading me—the way they're persuading all of us—to stay online longer, consume more media, and spend more money.

The same thing I saw happen with exotic, complex loans is happening all over again with technology and online marketing. Consumers are diving blind into situations that put them at risk. Nobody is explaining the risks and stakes in a way that is easy to understand.

I used to laugh off a silly impulse buy, but when I looked deep into this topic, I stopped laughing and I got angry. I am passionate about sharing this information with you. We can fight this, but first you have to know what we are fighting for. It all comes down to one disturbing truth: our ability to make free choices, our willpower, and our self-determination are under constant attack. These are not silly impulse buys. These are symptoms of the attack on our future.

VIRTUAL PUPPET MASTERS

We rely on the digital world for information, connection, and entertainment. Everyone knows that the internet and social media are ad-driven, and that they serve up customized search results to each user. But most people don't realize how deeply that "customization" takes advantage of their personal data, or how dangerously those search algorithms play on their emotions and primal, unconscious reactions. You are being brainhacked.

I hear clients and friends constantly beating themselves up: "I'm so stupid! I spend too much money. I waste too much time. I don't know what's wrong with me. I can't seem to break the cycle."

They feel helpless and out of control. They can't see the forces driving their behavior. They don't realize they're being swayed by technology that hacks directly into our deepest, instinctive behavior. They get sucked into a self-reinforcing illusion, and don't even know that the reality they see is created by their own choices.

Every time we click, we're building the world we live in. If you click on shoes, the algorithms will feed you more and more shoes until your screen is full of nothing else. Guess what? They also will feed you what people who liked those shoes also liked. The same thing happens when you click on cute puppies, or sad stories about suffering people, or angry rants about politics: before long, that's all you can see. And since gloom and doom hold our attention better than shoes or puppies, it doesn't take long for it to look as if the whole world is on fire.

What is that doing to us? What's it doing to our spending, our physical and mental health, and our relationships? What is it doing to our society?

Unconscious consumption affects every aspect of our waking lives—consumption of media, news, opinions, and above all, products. I want to pull back the curtain and show you all the ways you're being deceived and manipulated without your knowledge or consent.

There are a vast number of different people and companies who all want to put their hands in our wallets. They are chipping away at our financial freedom, and our consciousness, a fraction of a penny at a time. And we're playing along, clicking away our free choices. We're clicking away our grasp on objective reality. We're clicking away our futures, and the futures of our children.

I'm here to show you how to take back control, and use the power of technology to create the life—and the world—you really want. It is all within your grasp.

CUT THE STRINGS

This book is a self-defense guide to help you protect yourself from online predators of all stripes and position yourself for a positive financial (and emotional, and relational, and physical) future. You'll learn how the monetization of the internet through pay-per-click advertising turned a harmless communication platform into an out-of-control manipulation engine. We'll unpack the way algorithm-driven news and social media are dividing this country into toxic, warring mindsets. We'll examine how frictionless spending makes us impulsive, irrational, and broke. I'll share the latest research on all the ways marketers and tech giants are exploiting your brain biology to hack into your wallet. And we'll delve into all the ways that scammers and online influencers use social and emotional triggers to empty our bank accounts.

But don't worry—we won't stop there. I'll also show you practical steps to reclaim your attention and self-control. We'll explore creative ways that you can harness the power of big data and use it for good. We'll celebrate the richness of the beautiful, messy real world that no virtual construct can replicate. Ultimately, I'll teach you how to become a conscious consumer of media, a conscious consumer with your money, and a mindful participant in a better world.

MY VANTAGE POINT

As a mortgage lender, I am the person you call when you want to buy a house and need money. I spend eight to twelve hours, five days a week, talking to people about money—and their relationship with money. I have been doing this for fifteen years now. That's thousands upon thousands of conversations about money. We talk about money goals, money "sins" of the past, fears, and spending patterns. We put together financial game plans. I know people, and I know how our financial behavior connects to every other part of our lives.

I use YouTube, TikTok, Facebook, Instagram, and LinkedIn to reach and educate new clients and grow my business. As one of the earlier adopters of social media for my business, I have watched it grow, and watched people's relationship with social media and technology change. I have seen the financial impact of social media use increase year by year as technology has become faster, smarter, and even more focused on opening your wallet.

Most of all, I can tell you from speaking with all these thousands of people, and watching the changes in technology and society, that there has been a seismic shift in the way we are being sold to—how we're sold products, aspirations, and beliefs. Five years ago, if I asked someone how often they received a package without remembering what was inside, they'd be offended. They'd think I was crazy.

Now they laugh and say, "Nine came this morning!" Mindless spending has been normalized into a joke that we bond over. Technology has changed the way we spend money and think about our spending. We have been brainhacked.

FIGHT THE GOOD FIGHT

You need to know up front, the one thing you won't find in this book is a political agenda. Anytime you talk about money, power, or the media, somebody will try to point fingers and bring party politics into the conversation. This book isn't a love letter to any political party, because they're all using the same tricks. This isn't an alarmist conspiracy theory. This is the reality of what happens with technological progress—everybody's trying to make a buck, these tools make them way, *way* too good at it, and the long-term collateral damage is catastrophic.

I'm also not about to suggest that you cancel your Amazon Prime membership, delete Facebook to avoid all their ads, and never go online again. That's not realistic. The moment your local grocery store runs out of toilet paper, where else are you going to look but the internet? Social media, online shopping, and streaming media are here to stay, and we have to learn how to live with them without losing our shirts—or our minds.

The information about online exploitation is out there. The terrible impacts of social media are public knowledge too. We've been having congressional hearings about them for years. But the data and testimony we're hearing is nearly impossible for the average person to grasp. It's full of scientific jargon and political doubletalk that obscures the truth.

The purpose of this book is to drill down into that data, translate it into ordinary language, and say, "Here's exactly how they are hacking your brain, and it's about to get worse. Here's what you can do about it." In order for you to understand how big tech trains your brain to spend, you also need to grasp the bigger context of all the different, damaging ways tech manipulates our thinking and behavior. I want you to see for yourself how marketers are using technology to change the way you think, feel, and the way you spend. I want you to *really* understand why you're spending what you're spending. I want you to understand that there's an enemy in your phone (or laptop, or desktop, or watch) that you aren't prepared to face, and it isn't a fair fight.

I'm going to share some of my deepest, darkest, embarrassing secrets about how I've been brainhacked myself. I'll also tell you how I got free, and you can too. Some of the truths I'm going to share are uncomfortable, or even scary. That's okay! You should be scared. But don't shy away. Ignorance is the enemy, and this information is empowering. You can make significant and lasting changes for the better. You can help others change too. We don't have to accept this as the new norm. We do not have to accept that tech is going to open our wallets and literally rewire our brains. We do not have to accept that privacy is a thing of the past. It's time to fight back!

There is so much at stake here. The battle for your dollars, for your attention, for your *brain*, impacts every aspect of your life. It affects your physical and mental health. It affects your relationships and your participation in society. It affects the way you prepare for your future, as well as the future of our nation and our world. We need to fight for our hard-earned money, for our time, for our sanity, and for the kind of world we want our children to live in.

The battle starts in your own mind, and your weapon is knowledge. Suit up.

CHAPTER ONE

FROM MARKETING TO MENTALISM

"Advertising funded search engines will be inherently biased towards the advertisers and away from the needs of the consumers."

That quote is from a public statement by Google founders Larry Page and Sergey Brin.[1] They made it back in 1998, when Google was just a prototype they were introducing to the world. Back then, they intended it as a warning. They wanted Google to help build an internet that ran on high-quality information, not just sponsored marketing messages.

Well, they say the road to hell is paved with good intentions. Every technological advancement from that day to this has made that bias against consumers' best interests—*your* best interests—even worse.

The advertising you see all over your browser, email, and social media is just the tip of the iceberg. The real influence of marketing on every aspect of your life is nearly impossible to grasp completely. It's like peeling an onion—the layers just keep going. The sci-fi writer Arthur C. Clarke once said, "Any sufficiently advanced technology is indistinguishable from magic." The technology of brainhacking is incredibly advanced, and works very much like a magic trick—almost a form of hypnosis.

In order for you to understand what it means to be *brainhacked*—and why it's so dangerous—you need to understand three things up front:

1. what brainhacking is;
2. how brainhacking became the invisible architecture of everything you see, read, and watch online; and
3. how it affects you without you even knowing.

WHAT IS BRAINHACKING?

Take a look at the tech timeline at the end of this chapter. The internet was born as a noncommercial venture. It was created for military communication, expanded for academic use by universities, and then became a playground for hobbyists. For decades, it was a useful (and to some people, fascinating) tool.

By the early 1990s, technology infrastructure opened up for commercial use. Access to the World Wide Web became widely available to businesses, and to consumers with money to spend. That made it a juicy target for marketers. Soon marketing became the most lucrative use of this new technology, and money invested in online businesses accelerated the development of online technology.

In the last fifteen years, the advent of social media and

smartphones skyrocketed the amount of money to be made online—*made from you*. And therefore, the amount of effort being directed at parting you from your money has skyrocketed, as well.

The internet as we know it today exists for one reason, and one reason only: to capture, exploit, and sell your attention. Advertisers want to make money *from* you by selling you products and services. Search engines, platforms, and content creators want to make money *off of* you by collecting and selling your personal data, and by tracking and manipulating your behavior. Brainhacking is the sum of all that technology, psychology, neuroscience, and data collection put together. It doesn't just lead you to spend money. It makes you vulnerable to emotional, mental, and social side effects that are incredibly damaging.

It starts—as the Google founders predicted—with advertising. Now, people have always sold goods and services. They have always needed to attract buyers' attention and get them interested. **But technology has fundamentally altered the way advertising works. Instead of trying to catch your eye, today's marketers catch your brain.**

Traditional advertisers tried to get attention with images, humor, or shock value. They negotiated ad placements to reach a certain audience. They encouraged impulse spending with grocery store endcaps, magazines in the checkout aisle, and late-night infomercials.

In the early days of the internet, online advertising worked much the same way as offline advertising. Marketers used movement, imagery, and sound to grab your attention, like a sign-spinner dancing on the side of the road, or one of those inflatable wiggly-arm figures outside a used car dealership. This system had two huge problems:

- People hated the ads. They were a huge turn-off. This, of course, made search engines less useful and cut into their profits.
- Marketers could guess that people who were reading a particular website would be interested in related topics—but they couldn't know for sure. They basically had to hold their breath and hope anyone noticed their ads.

The solution they came up with was what we now know as pay-per-click advertising (PPC). Instead of paying for the equivalent of a billboard sitting on the side of the road, the advertiser would only pay when a user clicked on their ad. This addressed both problems—it changed the way ads were designed, to be enticing instead of merely distracting. It also tracked user behavior so advertisers could know instantly how well the ad was working.

Then, they added a third element: tying advertisements to keywords in users' searches. Advertisers could bid on certain words and phrases related to their products so their ads would be shown to people who were already in a frame of mind to buy. Enter Bill Gross and his company GoTo.com in 1998 (later renamed Overture). Overture put it all together: combining keyword-driven search results with PPC ads. This approach was so successful that Yahoo bought Overture for $1.63 billion in 2003. That's right—*billion*, with a *b*.[2]

So, it goes like this:

1. Advertisers bid to link their ads to keywords.
2. Search engines serve up the ads to users who search for those terms.
3. The ads are designed to encourage users to click.
4. Then the advertiser pays for each click they get.

Remember that sequence. Remember the billions. They matter.

THE PRICE OF ATTENTION

Keyword-driven PPC sounds like a great idea, on the face of it. Advertisers waste less money. Ads don't need to be distracting and annoying, because they're advertising something the user was looking for anyway. Users don't have to bother with a bunch of irritating ads they don't care about. Win, win, win, right?

Wrong. So very wrong.

To make PPC work, software developers had to invent a whole new technology—a search algorithm—that could track bids, searches, and clicks, and use that information to change the search results (and the ads served) on the fly. **This shift in technology changed the whole economic foundation of the internet. Eventually, it changed the economics of every kind of media.**

Suddenly, the internet created a completely new commodity out of thin air: user engagement. Just like gold, silver, oil, or coffee, user engagement can be measured, priced, and bought in quantity. Instead of selling *space* (like on a billboard or in a magazine), the companies serving up PPC ads could package and sell *your actions, your attention, in real time.* A whole new industry was born to study, analyze, and manipulate the human brain on a massive scale.

It's the brainhacking industry. The industry exists to take away your free will and turn your behavior into a commodity. The way that industry works, and the fallout for all of our lives—that's what this whole book is about.

WHY IS BRAINHACKING *EVERYWHERE*?

Short answer: because the more ads you see, the more money there is to be made. And we're talking about *a lot* of money.

Google started selling ads in the year 2000, with about 350 advertisers that year. Today there are more than seven million advertisers using Google PPC. Two out of every five small or midsized businesses run some kind of PPC campaign. They are bidding for spots on any one of the forty thousand search queries Google processes *every second*, many of which come from consumers looking for a product or a product review.[3]

Google lets advertisers choose which search terms they want their ad to show up on—their keywords. Advertisers can also pinpoint the age, race, gender, and income of the people they want to see the ad, what time of day they want the ad to show up, and even what type of device the consumer should be using.[4] If the advertiser's ideal customer is a fifty-five- year-old man in Wisconsin shopping for a used 2019 Ford F150 in the middle of the night on their Android phone, that's exactly when and where it will appear.

Apple, Microsoft, and your favorite social media platforms all have similar programs. Social media often has more intensely targeted advertising options because they have more data on you. You spend a lot of time there, so they know you like a "bestie" would. That knowledge is gold to advertisers. Ever wondered why Facebook wanted so badly to know your big life moments? Dollar bills.

You are surrounded by PPC ads anytime you go online. They may appear off to the side of the content and have a "sponsored" label. They could stream right in the content flow like TikTok. They can even appear in your direct messages. Fifty years ago, the average consumer in the US saw about five hundred ads a day, primarily in printed products like newspapers and magazines, or ads running on television. Nowadays, we are bombarded with anywhere from four thousand to ten thousand marketing messages a day.[5]

How much money are we talking about? Billions every year.

The top three advertising platforms are Google, Facebook, and Amazon. In 2021, 80 percent of all companies using PPC ads used Google Ads.[6] Google accounted for an estimated 28.6 percent of all digital advertising revenue in the United States. Facebook and Amazon followed, with 23.8 and 11.3 percent each.[7]

Google Ads sold $209 billion in PPC ads in 2021.[8] Facebook's ad revenue in the US was $114.9 billion.[9] Amazon earned $32 billion in ad revenue.[10]

The stakes are high, and with that much money flowing around, everyone wants a piece of it.

KEYWORDS DRIVE CONTENT

There are two sides to the keyword-advertising equation: the advertiser and the content provider. After all, nobody goes online just to look at ads! Most of the time you're looking for information, news, entertainment, or a social connection. Those content providers are in business to make money, so they need to host advertisements.

Advertisements are linked to keywords, remember? Search engines place sites that have those keywords higher up in the search results. Content providers learned that if they had the right keywords on their webpage, they got more user engagement. More user engagement = more money.

In a nod to their founders' warning, Google doesn't just sell keywords to the highest bidder. In 2005, they introduced Quality Scores. Google vets each ad's relevance, including the quality of the advertiser's landing page. The higher the Quality Score, the less an advertiser will pay, and vice versa—advertisers with low Quality Scores pay a much higher price. (This is supposed to make it harder for shady advertisers to game the system. As we'll see, that doesn't always work out the way it's supposed to.) In the same way, a web page that's just a list of keywords with nothing interesting or useful to say isn't going to earn a good spot in the search results. They'll get marked down for low quality.

But, like I told you up front, every technological change that was supposed to make the internet better has wound up making it worse: in order to show up in searches, content providers have to use keywords. They can't just list those keywords. They have to embed them into the content in ways that look natural. They have to make content about certain topics *just so they can use the keywords.* This type of content manipulation is called Search Engine Optimization (SEO).

Advertising and SEO wove themselves together more and more tightly. Marketing became content. Content became marketing. And even though advertisers don't directly tell content providers what they should create and publish, they still control the narrative—because advertisers bid on the keywords, making them more valuable. Content providers are rewarded for being sneaky, and punished for ignoring keywords. And the constant of human nature is that whatever you reward, you get more of.

Interesting content that features valuable keywords makes money. So SEO became a vital part of blogging, news, entertainment, and online visibility. Even content providers who aren't trying to make money—charities, churches, political causes, arts organizations, and other nonprofits—have to use SEO to get their message seen. It's the way the system works now.

Sites with news feeds that used to show content in chronological order as it was posted changed to show the content that was most popular, or that was "suggested for you" based on your history. Everything became trackable and traceable. **As soon as clicks became dollars, the massive success of that system gradually turned everything into clickbait.**

PERCEPTION WITHOUT AWARENESS

To best explain how brainhacking affects you on a subconscious level, let's take a closer look at magic tricks. After all, they work very much the same way. British magician and mentalist Derren Brown specializes, as he puts it, in "magic, suggestion, psychology, misdirection, and showmanship." His performances often include a reveal segment, where he shows how the trick was done and explains how fake psychics, pickpockets, or scammers use the same techniques.

In 2009, he produced a TV show called *How to Control the Nation*.[11] In it, he demonstrates the phenomenon of Perception Without Awareness: the way our minds are influenced or "primed" to accept certain ideas by repeated exposure to images, music, or words and phrases that seem coincidental and fly under the radar of our consciousness. In one especially fun segment, he appears to magically predict which toy a volunteer would choose out of a large toy store—a little giraffe plushie—and even what name she would decide to give it.

When he reveals the trick, it turns out that he'd planted images of giraffes and giraffe-patterned spots all along her route to the store and around the store itself. The ceiling was decorated with letters that spelled out "giraffe," there were giraffe-themed books displayed on the shelves, and he'd salted his whole conversation with subtle hints, references, and gestures that suggested the image to her. She never noticed any of these things consciously because he kept her attention occupied with silly tasks and a stream of patter. Her unconscious mind noticed, and responded exactly the way he wanted her to. A study of Brown's work published in 2020 by the National Academy of Sciences confirmed the effectiveness of unconscious psychological priming on large numbers of people.[12]

It doesn't work on everybody, all the time. But it works on enough people, enough of the time, to make a lot of marketers very rich.

Today, the whole online world is that toy store, and unconscious priming appears everywhere. Sophisticated marketing campaigns salt celebrity gossip and interviews into the media to generate interest in a TV show long before it's released. Our searches and clicks allow advertisers to latch onto our browsers and follow us everywhere we go, presenting the same products over and over. We are beyond the point of being manipulated and sold to by advertising. Our thoughts, feelings, and actions are being bought and sold every time we share a joke, watch a movie or a how-to video, read a news article, or connect with friends and family on social media.

Mr. Brown's special is available on his YouTube channel, and you should check it out. As a fun game for extra credit, notice what other videos the algorithm will suggest for you after you watch it. Pay attention to the ads too. Write them down and then review: what do the algorithms think you are interested in? Are they right? And no, do not buy anything from those ads!

MINDLESS CONSUMPTION

Digital media is everywhere, and it's always on. That means that we are being marketed to—lulled into Perception Without Awareness—twenty-four hours a day. And whether we realize it or not, we often respond to the stimulus of that marketing by spending our money unnecessarily—even unconsciously. Like a hypnotic trance, we can still react to the world around us, but without conscious thought behind our actions.

I'm not immune to this magic trick myself—I fall for it *all the time.* Let me give you a real-life example: I love to collect poster-art prints. Shepard Fairey is one of my favorites. His posters look great framed, can be thought-provoking, and I'm always excited when a new one is released. Recently I bought one and took it to my regular framer. As I took it out of its tube, the woman at the counter gave me an odd look. Some of what I buy definitely deserves that look, but in this case, it was fairly tame. I was puzzled. She could tell I had no idea why she was staring at me with bewilderment.

"Jen, we're framing this one for you already. I'm working on it right now."

"What are you talking about?" I asked. "This one's brand new."

She pointed to the back room, laughing. "Yeah, well, it was brand new the first time you brought it in too."

Turns out, I had bought the same print twice in the same month without even realizing it. Even worse, it was not the first time I'd done that. This is a prime example of what it means to become an unconscious consumer: someone who makes unnecessary purchases without a second thought—and often, without even a memory of having done so. I couldn't tell you how or where I might have been "primed" to buy. I'm just so ingrained in the habit of collecting that I never questioned it.

"Hold on!" you might be thinking. "This has never happened to me. I know where all my money goes!" A decade ago, that might've been easy enough to verify. Back then, if a friend said to me, "I can't figure out where I'm spending my money," I could sit them down and see if they were overspending on their cell phone, internet, cable, eating out, Starbucks—the usual suspects. The whole process was really easy and simple.

These days, unconscious consumption can be tough to nail down.

THE UNHACKING CHALLENGE

As you go through this book, I'll offer you a series of challenges to help you unhack your brain. The first challenge is all about awareness, so here are some quick questions to help you recognize your own hypnotic purchases:

1. In the last year, have you had a package show up to your door without knowing what was inside? When you opened it, did you suddenly remember buying it for the first time?
2. Name every recurring subscription you currently have. Seriously, try it.
3. If you believe you were successful at question 2, check your credit card and bank statements. Did you really get them all?
4. In the last three years, have you read any news articles—perhaps regarding the pandemic or natural disasters—that led you to stock up on emergency items? Did you end up needing that full cache, or in your panic, did you overbuy? Let me remind you of the toilet paper craze of 2020. Did you stock up?
5. Have you ever forgotten that you ordered something and then bought it again? Or ordered an item, never noticed when it didn't show up, and only remembered when you reviewed your credit card statement?

If you answered yes to any of these questions, then you—like most of us—have become an unconscious consumer. You'll get zero judgment from me—I constantly have to force myself awake, to become aware of my own actions and responses. And if you're anything like me, you're now eager to understand how and why you got hacked in the first place—which brings us back to user engagement.

Unconscious consumption isn't just about buying *stuff*. It's also about the content you're consuming and messages you absorb about the world. So, when that content is created for the single goal of increasing user engagement, and stuffed with keywords chosen by advertisers, what kind of magic spell are you falling under?

Spoiler alert: it ain't good.

THE RISE OF THE MACHINES

A timeline of technology and why it is now impacting your wallet:

- 1969: The US Department of Defense launches ARPANET, a network of computers linked over telephone lines.[13]
- 1980: Graduate students develop USENET, a network of computer messaging systems for academic use. Cable News Network (CNN) launches, popularizing 24/7 news coverage of national and world events. The *Columbus Dispatch* becomes the first digital newspaper, offering access through a direct dial-up connection (the service could not display ads, pictures, or comics).[14]
- 1982: Telenet, the first commercial computer network, allows international email communication.
- 1985: The first domain name is registered under the Domain Name System (DNS). A commercial internet provider, PlayNET, launches—later renamed America Online (AOL).
- 1990: The Uniform Resource Locator (URL) system and hypertext markup language (HTML) create the first standardized version of the World Wide Web (the current format of www.domainname.com).
- 1994: The first online advertisement appears. AT&T pays $30,000 to place a banner on the magazine site Hotwired. com, as part of its futuristic "Have You Ever? You Will."

marketing campaign. The ad leads to a virtual tour of art museums all over the world—but nothing to buy immediately. Approximately 44 percent of people who see it click on it.[15]

- 1995: Internet Explorer, Amazon, Yahoo, and eBay all launch. AOL has about three million users.[16]
- 1997: A standard Wi-Fi networking protocol is released for commercial use.[17]
- 1998: Page and Brin publish their description and prototype of a new artificial intelligence-driven search engine, Google. GoTo.com launches its keyword-based advertising system.
- 1999: Apple releases the first mass-produced consumer device with Wi-Fi capabilities, the iBook laptop.[18]
- 2001: AOL merges with the media company Time Warner to create a mega-conglomerate of news, entertainment, and online content providers. The same year, cell phones with internet connectivity hit the market, allowing users to send and receive email or perform simple searches.
- 2003: Friendster, a social networking site, launches. It gains three million users within the first year.[19]
- 2004: The social network MySpace is the most-visited website on the planet.[20] "The facebook" (as it was called at the time) is invented as a network for Harvard University students only.[21] More US internet users have access to broadband than dial-up connections—speeds are faster, and the average person no longer has to choose between using the internet and using the phone.
- 2006: Facebook opens to the public, for anyone over age thirteen.[22]
- 2007: Twitter launches, calling itself a "microblogging" platform.[23] The smartphone era begins, as the iPhone is unveiled, and Google announces that its own mobile operating system,

Android, will be freely available for device manufacturers to develop products.[24]

- 2008: Rates of anxiety and depression in American adults begin a ten-year upward trend.[25]
- 2010: Instagram launches. It is distinguished from other social media sites as a mobile-only app, without desktop functionality. It gains one million users in its first two months.[26] In the US, 35 percent of households have a smartphone, and 10 percent have a tablet.[27]
- 2011: Snapchat launches. It is unique in that photos and messages disappear shortly after being opened. Later features allow photos and videos to be saved for twenty-four hours.
- 2012: Facebook acquires Instagram for $1 billion. Facebook reaches one billion registered users. The use of AI "bots" on social media is so prevalent that researchers begin to study how to distinguish bot from human activity.[28] Forty-five percent of US adults own a smartphone.[29]
- 2016: Voice Over Internet Protocol (VOIP) is so prevalent that for the first time, over half of Americans (50.8 percent) do not have a landline phone at all.[30] Social media becomes a major influence in the US presidential campaign. Over the next two years, bombshell revelations about illegal data harvesting by the firm Cambridge Analytica, and manipulation of public sentiment by foreign cyberattackers and social media bots, shake public confidence in the US political system.[31]
- 2018: Seventy-seven percent of US adults own a smartphone.[32] Studies reveal that rates of anxiety and depression in American adults are up 84 percent for younger adults and 30 percent overall, since 2008.[33]
- 2020: During the first year of the COVID-19 pandemic, the increase in global computer use is estimated between 10 per-

cent[34] and 70 percent.[35] Rates of anxiety and depression jump 25 percent globally.[36]

- 2021: Worldwide, 4.9 billion people use the internet—that's 63 percent of the world's population.[37] Facebook announces its name change to Meta, along with a new push to popularize the metaverse as its primary online platform.[38]

CHAPTER TWO

CHASING ENGAGEMENT

Advertisers want your clicks. To get your clicks, they must get your trust—which means they need to make you believe they're offering something of value. With billions of dollars at stake, it's not surprising that corporations are willing to push ethical boundaries.

What might that look like? Let's take the algorithm for a little test drive and find out.

I'm a mortgage lender. I do a lot of education for veterans about VA loans. So right now, I'm going to conduct a quick search using the term "VA mortgage." My first two hits are Veterans United and My Consumer Affairs. Your top results will be different, because Google doesn't serve up exactly the same ads or search hits on every computer. But I'm willing to bet your top ads and top search results will be pretty similar.

Veterans United is a mortgage company. They offer VA loans. So far, so good.

How about result number two? With a name like My Consumer Affairs, it looks to the untrained eye like a nonprofit or government-run consumer-advocate group. But when you click into their site, you see that it's simply a list of VA mortgage companies—or more accurately, a list of ads that My Consumer Affairs gets paid to host. There's no advocacy here. It's just a shell site selling leads to mortgage companies. Deceptive to say the least.

That's not all. As a lender myself, I notice that this list is headed by incredibly tempting, low mortgage rates—rates that, as far as I can tell from my end, not a single advertised company actually offers. Now, you may immediately say, "They can't do that! It's illegal!"

Well...sites like this do the bare minimum to stay compliant with regulations. And frankly, there are just too many sites out there for the authorities to police them all. If their quoted rates turn out to be wrong, they don't have much to lose. In most states, they aren't liable for it. The lender who advertises with them *might* be liable. But they have a built-in defense: how could the lender *possibly* be responsible for their advertiser's "computer glitch"?

Sites like this (and there are plenty, like top10bestlenders.com, bestonlinemortgageloan.com, consumersadvocate.com, and the list goes on) are marketing lead generators. They get paid a fee to collect consumer information and send it to mortgage companies. Their ratings, rankings, and recommendations have nothing to do with the quality or trustworthiness of the lenders they show you—the rankings just show how much the lenders paid for a slot.

In Chapter One, we talked about how content providers are rewarded for being sneaky about embedding keywords into their content. It goes further than that. **Content providers are rewarded for lying to you.**

Hold that thought.

ENGAGEMENT IS EMOTIONAL

Every time you look at a Facebook photo, a YouTube video, a news article—anything posted to an ad-supported site—that content exists because the site owners want you to click ads and make them money. I'm not suggesting that your friends and family post photos on Facebook because *they* want you to spot that Wayfair ad flashing next to Cousin Julie's new baby photos. But Facebook and Wayfair sure do. That slot next to those baby pictures is high-dollar real estate for a very good reason: your emotions.

Over the years, advertisers have learned something key about human behavior: we take action (like clicking or buying) based on emotions, not logic. The specific ads appearing on your screen are anything but random. Host platforms make huge investments into developing artificial intelligence to track your online activity, build a profile of you as a consumer, and assault you with exactly the ads that are most likely to push your emotional buttons. Emotional reactions = engagement. Engagement = money. So to marketers, emotional reactions = money.

The thing is, the algorithms that make money off your engagement don't care what *kind* of emotions they're evoking, as long as they are strong enough to make you click and buy. The stronger, the better. Warm fuzzies over baby pictures or old friends are one thing. Depression, fear, and anxiety can motivate you even more powerfully. This is why click-driven content algorithms have spawned clickbait news. A decade or so ago, you could read an article online and know from context whether the source and content were dependable. These days, not so much—all because news sites make more money by chasing your clicks than by producing thoughtful, high-quality news. That usually means one thing: negativity.

IF IT BLEEDS, IT LEADS

As human beings, we all give more weight to negative information or events than to the positive. Psychologists refer to this as a "negativity bias."[39] It might be a primitive survival mechanism—if you miss seeing a flower, you'll never know the difference. If you miss seeing a saber-toothed tiger, you're dead.

Brainhackers use this negativity bias to chase user engagement, and the news media is a prime outlet. After all, if you see the headline, "Man Saves Baby from Swimming Pool," you'll be happy. But will you click through to read the story? Probably not. But if you see the headline, "Serial Rapist Terrorizes Neighborhood," you'll want to know *what* neighborhood! Is it yours? You're going to click the link to make sure you or your loved ones aren't in danger.

The news media has always been ad-supported and favored negative headlines. As long as those ads were based on circulation or viewership, there was value in presenting balanced stories. Those days are gone.

Newspaper circulation peaked in the mid-1970s, and held fairly steady to around 1990. With the rise of 24/7 television news and internet news outlets, newspaper circulation (and journalistic standards) began a long decline. Between 2008 and 2021, about half the journalists in the country lost their jobs. Digital advertising helped shore up revenue for traditional news publishers, but it couldn't break the industry's fall.[40]

The largest and most well-established newspapers, like the *New York Times*, the *Washington Post*, and the *Los Angeles Times*, tried to staunch the bleeding by putting their content behind a paywall. Today, nearly 80 percent of US newspapers with circulation higher than fifty thousand have some sort of paywall for their online content.[41] But they find themselves in a real pickle: since they've decimated their news staff, they struggle to produce a quality product that people are willing to pay for. And with so many online news outlets providing stories for free, readers aren't convinced the content is worth anything anyway.

How do those free news outlets earn their keep? Through PPC ads and keyword-driven content. Fear and clickbait. That constant drum of negative news affects us all, as we see in another huge trend: **anxiety rates for American adults under fifty increased 30 percent between 2008 and 2018. When you look at just the 18- to 25-year-old group, that increase was 84 percent over those ten years.**[42] **In 2020 alone, rates of anxiety and depression jumped 25 percent worldwide.**[43]

News outlets aren't *trying* to make people suffer. They aren't thinking about our nation's mental health or stability at all. They are businesses trying to increase their profits.

Go ahead—get on your phone and scan Apple News, Google News, or your preferred platform. Which of the top headlines are you most tempted to click? How many are anything but negative? What view of the world does this create? How does this make you feel?

THE RISE OF FAKE NEWS

As we've seen, news organizations have every incentive to slant the news to the bad, which naturally slants our worldviews as well. It's not that you want to believe that dirty bombs and human trafficking are on the rise—but if you click such headlines once, you're teaching all those sophisticated algorithms to feed you more. And who wouldn't feel their worldview darkening under a steady diet of negativity and pain?

And, just like the example of misleading mortgage rates, the algorithm doesn't care whether all the news it shows you is *true*. The only thing that matters is getting you to click. So, journalists aren't rewarded for publishing balanced news—just for playing on your negative emotions. And they aren't rewarded for being accurate—just for being provocative. The result? **The truth is in trouble.**

This method of shifting public perception is so effective that it's upended the world of politics. Both the Democrat and Republican parties have funded organizations that pose as legitimate local news outlets, just to push a particular message—or even produce hit pieces about their political opponents. You'll hear both sides complain about "fake news." They're both right.

In 2020, the Nieman Journalism Lab at Harvard University

tracked the growth of more than four hundred partisan media outlets funded by government officials, political candidates, political action committees, and party operatives. They were popping up all over the country, with both left-and right-leaning agendas—mostly in swing states.

There's big business in these "local" news sites, but many weren't even located in the cities they supposedly covered. One of the founders, Brian Timpone, used to operate "local news" sites in the US produced by writers in the Philippines using fake bylines.[44] His Chicago-based group, Locality Labs, ran a network of at least 450 "local" news sites distributed across Michigan, Illinois, and Maryland.

The *New York Times* also looked at the proliferation of these "fake news" sites. In 2019, they found that partisan political action committees (PACs) would pay for Locality Labs and other remote outlets to publish articles about their favored candidates, and then pay the website to mail copies of the articles to voters—without identifying them as political ads. Other so-called news sites didn't even have any staff listed. They turned out to be run entirely by political activists and commentators—even though they didn't disclose their funding as PACs are required to do.[45] A former writer for Locality Labs coined the phrase "pink slime journalism" to refer to the mashup of tidbits of real news with plenty of artificial filler, mass-produced by an industrial-sized extruding machine.[46]

The FCC regulates television advertising, so if these online pieces were TV ads, they'd have to be more transparent about their funding: "This message is paid for by the campaign to reelect Mayor Jane Doe." But online news sources are exempt from FCC rules, so they have no such restrictions. A political party can simply assign the writer a series of talking points and watch the sparks turn to flame.

For example, say an article goes out claiming that our hypothetical Jane Doe's opponent, John Smith, got a DUI when he was sixteen. It won't take long for this headline to gain traction on Facebook, Twitter, and other social media. And because it's massively negative, and therefore massively clickable, more "legitimate" news outlets will soon begin reporting the story— or at least reporting that it's being reported. The attention the article has received now becomes the story, while its truthfulness takes a backseat. This is how unsubstantiated hit pieces go viral, all in the name of gathering PPC dollars.

What's the scam here? It's simple. According to the 2018 Poynter Media Trust Survey, Americans trust local reporting far more than national reporting.[47] Politicians are trying to take advantage of our trust in local news by creating fake local news organizations to "mudsling" and change voters' minds. It is propaganda dressed up as legitimate news from a local source. It's worked so far, but with these sites multiplying and the quality of newsrooms declining, how long do you think it's going to last? At this point, your average consumer can hardly be blamed for thinking news organizations aren't to be trusted—or that the world is falling to pieces around them.

And with all this digital mudslinging, guess what doesn't get campaign dollars, public awareness, and political will devoted to it? That's right—the regulation of big tech. Can you imagine the kind of bipartisan support that could be generated for effective oversight if the average American *really* understood how they were getting played? But of course, effective oversight is exactly what tech companies don't want.

CONNECTING THE DOTS

Clickbait, whether it's cheesy and obvious or sophisticated and subtle, is the financial backbone of major search engines, social media platforms, online gaming options, news outlets, and more. Let's take a moment to review where we've been so we can see clearly where we're going:

- The invention of PPC ads created a whole new economy around buying and selling human behavior (engagement).
- The monetization of clicks—a split-second, reflex response— drove marketers toward more and more covert, manipulative techniques.
- At the same time, businesses and content creators who need to reach new customers or audience members learned to

pack their content with valuable keywords and enticing headlines.

- Because clicks = cash, content providers are rewarded for lying, as long as they get attention.
- Negativity attracts the most clicks, so news media in particular is slanted heavily toward the dark and depressing, giving consumers the false idea that the world is worse off than ever.

So, what does this have to do with unconscious spending? It's simple. The more anxious and depressed you are, the more likely you are to spend on impulse. **Impulse spending is an emotional coping mechanism.**

Psychologists have long recognized emotional spending as a (potentially self-destructive) coping mechanism, similar to getting drunk or overeating. People experiencing depression and anxiety are more likely to make impulse purchases, trying to assuage their fears or raise their moods.[48] Ever heard of "retail therapy"? It's a real thing. It's not good for you. Just like overindulging in sugar, junk food, or booze, it gives you a short-term boost with long-term consequences.

THE SLIPPERY SLOPE

To add fuel to the spending fire, buying things online has become ridiculously easy. The industry term is "frictionless purchasing."

BJ Fogg, creator of the Behavior Design Lab at Stanford, wrote a book called *Tiny Habits: The Small Changes That Change Everything*[49] that delves into the psychology behind coding and developing choices. The basic premise developers are working with is this: if something's easy to do, you're more likely to do it.

The goal is to remove anything that might slow down the money leaving your wallet—removing friction.

For instance, the first time you buy something online, you have to get off the couch, find your wallet, and punch in your credit card number, one digit at a time. It's kind of a pain in the butt. You probably won't bother doing it unless you *really* want or need something. And it takes a couple of minutes, so the whole time you're going through the process, you could stop and think, "Is this really worth the money?"

But then you get the option to store your credit card info on the website for future purchases. You can even store it in your browser or phone, to autofill on any website. Whoosh. Any natural resistance to buying is erased, freeing you up to click-click-buy in three seconds flat. Are you fully considering a purchase if it only takes three seconds? Are you even going to remember that purchase?

Between emotional manipulation and the sheer ease of online shopping, the internet has taken impulse buying to a whole new level. Feeling anxious over the wildfires in California? Calm yourself by ordering five quadruple packs of fire extinguishers. Put on a few extra COVID pounds? Better buy some body bands, free weights, and diet pills. These small, emotionally driven purchases can add up quickly, draining our bank accounts of thousands—or even more. As a mortgage lender, I'm constantly seeing clients make questionable financial choices they never would have made a few years ago. They read articles saying that the COVID pandemic will never end, and they take over-the-top vacations—or worse, buy cars and "toys" they can't afford—because they figure, "Hey, I might as well go out in style."

With each click, we shape both our online and real worlds. We incentivize developers and content creators to mislead, manipulate, and frighten us into click-click-clicking in a constant search for uplift, peace, and satisfaction. They make us feel bad so they can make money from our constant engagement, and we spend money to make ourselves feel better. Brainhacking might be the root of this problem—but by continually fertilizing that root, we strengthen the vicious cycle that traps us.

THE REPROGRAM YOUR ADS CHALLENGE

You might look at online games, social media platforms, and advertisers and think, "What's the big deal if they watch my clicks? Let them spy on my boring life." But that's the thing: they're not just spying—they're using that intelligence to probe deeper and deeper into your psyche so they can better lure you into putting your money into their pockets. Unfortunately, there's no denying that PPC and the algorithms that serve it are powerful, lucrative, and here to stay. So if we can't remove manipulative marketing from our lives completely, what can we do?

The first step is simple—if these hosting platforms are paid by the click, then *stop clicking*. Here's a new seven-day challenge:

- **Day One**: Don't click a single ad. Nada. Zip.
- **Day Two**: Don't "like" or comment on any social media posts, photos, articles—anything.
- **Day Three**: Randomly search for an item you do not care about at all. For example, I *hate* crowds and loud noises. Music festivals are my idea of hell. If I search for "music festivals near me," guess what happens? I'll get ads for exactly what I can't stand. Choose topics you dislike or things that are irrelevant and make no sense. Are you a cat lover who

hates snakes? Search for boa constrictors. Hate the cold? Search ski vacations. Allergic to wool? Search for wool. Have fun with it.

· **Days Four through Seven**: As you see ads pop up for things you hate, click on a few of them. (Do **not**, under any circumstances, click on any ads that you actually think are interesting.)

By the end of the week, you'll leave all that artificial intelligence with a great big question mark over its head. You'll be on your way to freeing yourself from brainhacking hypnosis, and all its insidious side effects.

I often wonder if the creators of pay-per-click and keyword auctions ever look back and recognize the fallout of their work. Did they foresee the social, emotional, and financial consequences of their creations? Do they recognize or regret them now? In reality, it doesn't matter. Unintended consequences are still consequences—hitting someone with your car might be an accident, but that doesn't make their legs any less broken.

At this point, the real question is, how are those consequences affecting you? In the next chapter, we'll be diving deeper into the effect of click-driven algorithms on media, as well as the skewed social and financial narratives that shape how we all live. Remember, the algorithm doesn't care what you believe. It is only pushing your buttons so you will click links. That reflex response has pushed all of us further away from each other, and created a growing divide in our society.

CHAPTER THREE

———

THE GROWING DIVIDE

"The issue of social media is roughly the following: Social media have their—these are businesses, and their job is to maximize shareholder return and revenue. And the best way to maximize revenue is to maximize engagement. And the best way to maximize engagement in social media is with outrage, literally outrage on the left or the right.

These systems naturally push you to the extremes. And they do so for engagement reasons, not because of some moral or social reason. That problem is an unsolved problem. And we need to address it."[50]

In this statement, Eric Schmidt, the former CEO of Google, described the division in our society perfectly. The algorithms that hack our brains push us all toward extremes. They amplify the most hardline voices of every group or opinion, and encourage arguing and conflict. *Which* extreme doesn't matter. It only matters that we stay charged up, because then we keep clicking. We keep making them money.

In order to understand the effects of brainhacking on our social relationships and civic participation, we need to build on what we've learned so far about the personal impact of online manipulation. In Chapter One, we covered how valuable your attention is, and how every company online wants a piece of it. In Chapter Two, we discussed how the quest for user engagement (and the money that comes with it) dictates the content we see online.

Now, let's talk about how that clickbait content drives a wedge right through the heart of our society, and turns people against each other. We are all getting sorted into echo chambers, and we're losing our ability to talk and listen to anyone with a different perspective. There are so many dangerous ramifications of social and political polarization, I couldn't possibly cover them all in a single book. We're focused here on the ways that online manipulation affects our money habits, and the great social divide can drive us to make terrible money choices too.

Case in point: it distorts our perspective on the options we have in life, and what's even possible for a normal person to accomplish with normal amounts of money. Recently, I posted a sixty-second video to TikTok explaining a classic strategy for building wealth through real estate. The concept was simple enough, and it's been a staple of US wealth-building for centuries:

- Buy a starter home and live there for a few years while saving for your next down payment.
- Buy a second home and move in. Keep your starter home as a rental. Because you lived in the starter home prior to renting, your mortgage will stay at a lower, "owner-occupied" rate, and your next home will require less money down.

- Continue this process, using each rental property as a source of income as you move up to your dream home.

Again, this was a sixty-second video about a centuries-old concept, not some shady get-rich-quick scheme. I certainly didn't invent it.

About half the comments were from viewers who either wanted to try this method, or who already had tried it, with great results. But the other half? Well...here's a sample:

> "Terrible moral choice. Hoard first time homebuyers' properties. I hope all your tenants stop paying rent."

> "Bad idea. This method creates mass shortages, particularly locking out first time home buyers."

> "The housing market is rigged! I can't believe you don't know this! Many families and disabled cannot buy a home!! Like the majority!"

For the record—and I say this as an expert with more than fifteen years in this field—the real threat to housing in America is institutional investors (corporations and investment funds) that buy up *hundreds of thousands* of residential properties. It's not your neighbor down the street renting out two houses.

In any case, this polarized response demonstrates our current national conversation around money. The popular narrative suggests that there's a hard split between the ambition of the Haves and the despair of the Have-Nots, a sense that in America, you're either born with wealth—and therefore every opportunity to buy property—or will never own a home at all.

That's not reality. The truth is more complex (as the truth usually is). If you want to protect your money, you must learn to see past the half-truths and bias to the full story beyond.

THE CRACKUP

As a mortgage lender, I certainly see a sharp divide in attitudes when home-buying hopefuls consult with me about their options. The first group see life as a glass half-full and are pro-active. Their meetings tend to go like this:

> Me: "Unfortunately, due to your credit score, you don't qualify right now."

> Half-Full: "Okay, great. What can I do to fix that?"

I give them a list of steps to achieve their goals. They come back six months, a year, or two years later to announce that they're ready. They've taken my advice, acted on it, and cleared their path. I'm always so happy and excited to see my clients accomplish their list so I can usher them to the finish line! It makes me feel like a proud mom. A mortgage loan and home ownership are in sight. It's not *easy*, but the steps are straightforward. Work the list, and it will work.

It's not so simple for members of the second group—the ones who see the glass half-empty and are reactive. Those conversations tend to go this way:

> Me: "Unfortunately, due to your credit score, you don't qualify right now."

Half-Empty: "I'll never qualify."

Me: "Look, all you have to do is... (simple steps to solve the issue)."

Half-Empty: "No, I knew I wouldn't qualify. Only rich people can buy houses."

Then they hang up on me.

I've seen these opposite scenarios play out literally hundreds of times. (And I have to say the level of reactiveness has increased dramatically in the last five years.) Does financial inequality exist in this country? Of course! It's also true that those who believe they can fix their credit usually wind up doing so. Those who are convinced it's hopeless don't even try. See? It's complex.

Why are people's perspectives split so sharply—and so rigidly? After all, both are given options to meet their goals. Paying off debt and improving your credit score might be intimidating, but as hundreds of my own clients have proven—some of them with very serious problems—it's not impossible. So, you could argue that reactive people simply aren't willing to take responsibility the way proactive people are. Right?

No. You *could* make that argument, but you shouldn't. That argument is itself part of the growing divide! It splits people into a "right type" and a "wrong type," and writes off the "wrong type" as hopeless. Ultimately, they are all *people*, with two different mindsets. The reactive perspective isn't a character flaw. It's a mental space that people get trapped in. Social media reinforces and perpetuates the trap. It's a vicious loop, and brainhacking makes it even harder to get out of.

DOWN THE RABBIT HOLE

Remember how our online worlds are built: one click at a time. If the media you're consuming is "Ten Reasons You'll Never Own a House," the algorithm will soon helpfully supply "Top Five Ways the Wealthy Are Preying On the Poor." If you go far enough down this road, you'll eventually reach the likes of "Why the Rich Want to Drink Your Baby's Blood." Algorithms are designed to feed and amplify your interests—they're not designed to deliver you correct or balanced information.

Humans have amazing survival instincts. We're hardwired to look out for danger. The world has always been full of disease, war, crime, and natural disasters. But in the past, the average person focused on the problems in their own life and community. News from around the world arrived in short summaries, on a fixed schedule. Now we are grazing at a 24/7 disaster buffet.

In our modern world of pandemics, wildfire, political upheaval, and environmental changes, the instinct to stay alert for danger often results in "doomscrolling" as we continually search our social media feeds for news that we have to evacuate, get another vaccine, or stay indoors all day because the air quality outside is hazardous. While it's often important that we follow the news during a crisis, it's also true that this behavior, referred to by psychologists as a "pattern of frequent monitoring," causes even more intense feelings of sadness, fear, anxiety, and anger. We're doing the very thing that makes us feel worse. And as our mood worsens, the more inclined we are to keep scrolling. This negative spiral does a whammy on our mental health. Not only do we feel heightened anxiety and depression, but our mundane personal worries—did my car payment get lost in the mail? Will I have to pay more in taxes this year?—often seem far worse than they really are.[51] Anxiety makes us doomscroll. Doomscrolling makes us anxious. Rinse and repeat.

Look back at the technology timeline at the end of Chapter One. If you see a bit of half-empty, reactive thinking in yourself, don't freak out. Many consumers have no idea how biased their media actually is, but they get so wrapped up in one point of view that they can't imagine the other side has merit. Again, keep in mind that content providers design their platforms to keep you glued to your screen. If fear, anxiety, or mindless rage do the trick, they will produce content to provoke exactly those feelings.

Unfortunately, we're all susceptible to these types of messages. We know that depression and anxiety worsen with social media use,[52] as well as online usage overall.[53] If you don't go online armed with good information and an understanding of how the system can manipulate you, falling down the rabbit hole is only too easy.

As an experiment, I recently released a YouTube video called "You're a Loser and You'll Never Own a House." The title was full-on clickbait. It's the exact *opposite* of my actual message. But because of that title, the video received a ridiculous number of views and it's still one of the top five videos on my channel.

To continue this experiment, I am filming a whole series of videos with extremely negative titles but really, *really* positive messages in the content. It will be interesting to see how this spins the mood. If you ask, the algorithm will deliver—so let's deliver some "glitter bombs" of sneaky joy hidden in the rage-bait and despair.

THE POISON PILL

The problem with hanging out too long in rabbit holes is that we start to think like rabbits. Our tastes change. We get tunnel vision. We get comfortable down there, and get uncomfortable with the outside world. In other words, the messages we receive shape our worldview—and we mistrust anyone or anything that doesn't fit. Let's go back to my TikTok for a moment. Remember, I had a ton of comments from people who used the same method and thought it was great. I also received dozens of insults from viewers convinced I was from a different planet—born into wealth and oblivious to the real world:

> "I think her old man owns the bank so she can get that primo deluxe credit."

> "How much money did your parents give you?"

I didn't take it personally. You could easily see what rabbit hole the viewer was in, based on their comments. I just hate to see a negative filter block people from taking good, practical advice.

"Rabbit holes" are nothing new. Brainhacking is just digging them deeper, faster. I recently read *Crystallizing Public Opinion* by Edward Bernays. He points out that individual media outlets select stories that will appeal to their base. Those choices are influenced by political agendas, marketers, and advertisers.

Guess when this book was published? A century ago: 1923.

Bear in mind, in 1923 the average person would read one newspaper, or maybe two. Collecting papers from other cities would cost a fortune, even if they could get them. But if they did (maybe at a public library), each paper would have a different perspective. The reader would constantly meet different points of view that balanced each other.

Today, we can easily access news stories from around the world—but they are all generated from the same press feeds (and often by the same newsrooms). They're chosen by the algorithm to match our preexisting beliefs. So those beliefs get stronger and stronger, reinforced by the illusion that "everyone" agrees with us.

PANDORA'S BOX

The tendency of online algorithms to push more and more extreme content has started creating problems for advertisers as well as consumers. The artificial intelligence that places ads on content has become self-directed to the point that advertisers aren't always happy with the results.

Decades ago, advertisers could easily influence media organizations to stay in line—or at least, not cast their brands in a bad light. But online, the keyword-driven ad machine operates in ways that neither the content creators nor the advertisers really understand, and often in ways they can't choose. As a result, advertisers have little to no direct influence over what content they appear alongside—even brands considered top-shelf in the United States, like Procter & Gamble, Walmart, Johnson & Johnson, Hershey, and Adidas.

In 2017 and again in 2018, several big-name companies discovered that their ads on YouTube were being run on channels they deemed inappropriate.[54] Some of the worst examples included terrorist recruitment and pedophilia. Obviously, they didn't choose these locations; algorithms did. But the content was so appalling that these companies worried their brands would be damaged by association.

Since then, YouTube has implemented a scoring system that requires content creators to certify that their material is suitable for advertisers, and it is reviewed automatically or by human moderators before it goes live with ads. So far, YouTube is the only platform with such a program. Facebook, Instagram, and TikTok all show ads, but without any disclosures about the content. With massive amounts of video and written content being uploaded every minute, from millions of different creators, platforms can't even enforce their own policies consistently, much less the advertisers' preferences. How ironic—advertisers bid on keywords, the keywords drive the content, and yet the content sometimes comes as a nasty surprise to the advertiser. **Advertising algorithms push such extreme content that advertisers are worried about their brands.**

We've spent a lot of time discussing how algorithms and advertisers feed us information that is biased, negative, and misleading. It's all too easy to find ourselves buried in rabbit holes that slant our worldview, damage our mental health, and influence our spending choices. So how do we change this?

With no effective way to monitor these content providers, you should question *any* media message that comes your way—especially when it comes to your money. And instead of allowing worries about the future to control your money choices now, you need to flip the script: learn for yourself how to make financial decisions that can give you a better future.

EDUCATE YOURSELF

The antidote to the poison pill of misinformation is good information. Unfortunately, most Americans didn't grow up with good information about money—also known as basic financial literacy. Financial literacy is a group of knowledge, attitudes, skills, and behaviors that help you make wise financial choices and be successful with money.[55]

Our rates of financial literacy in the US are *terrible*. **Most studies agree that just under half of Americans are financially literate.** The most recent National Financial Capability Study by the Financial Industry Regulatory Authority (FINRA) showed that only 40 percent of American adults could answer four out of six questions correctly on a basic financial knowledge quiz.[56]

If you're one of the other 60 percent, don't be embarrassed! You weren't taught. The insane fact is that most American students don't get any financial education at all. As I write this, only twenty-one states require all students to receive some kind of financial education in high school, but it can be very short or included as a unit with another class. Twenty-four states require schools to *offer* financial education, but students don't have to take it to graduate.[57] Just six states require high schoolers to complete a semester-long, stand-alone personal finance course.[58] Let me repeat that: *only six states require a whole semester of financial literacy.*

It has always boggled my mind the amount of time spent on topics we will never use in the real world, yet basic personal finance is considered cutting-edge. You have to learn another language, but not how to manage basic adult tasks like balancing your bank account, building credit, or planning for retirement?

Let me tell you how much my remedial French has helped with my finances: le z'ero.

Hopefully, the situation is changing. In 2021, about twenty-four state legislatures were considering bills to mandate financial education. Experts saw this as a result of the growing burden of student debt, but also a cultural upwelling of awareness about economic inequality exacerbated by the pandemic.[59] In this instance, social media may be a good thing, because it's shining a light on these issues.

Americans generally gain our money know-how from our parents, which is a big part of why poverty cycles exist: parents who lack financial knowledge can't pass on good habits to their children, so each generation slides further down the monetary pit. One standout exception occurred following the foreclosure crisis of 2008, when children saw their parents' finances ruined firsthand, then decided to educate themselves to avoid the same fate.

If you weren't lucky enough to have money-savvy parents guiding your financial education, it's time to follow the example of these "foreclosure kids." Find some good resources now, and study up. Let me emphasize this point—the internet (however treacherous) is full of fantastic, reputable resources. The difference is that you have to seek them out instead of accepting whatever the algorithm spoon-feeds you. Often, would-be homeowners call me having already conducted hours of nuanced research on their own. Instead of feeling despondent that they'll never own a home, they are empowered to take the future into their own hands. My job becomes to simply confirm that the choices they've mapped out are smart ones. You can do the same.

I strongly recommend the work of Suze Orman and Dave Ramsey to study basic financial literacy on your own. They give solid education with plenty of motivational gusto. I would caution you to take some of Dave's advice with a grain of salt (like the fact that you do actually need to maintain a credit rating instead of disappearing from the grid with a cash-only lifestyle). But overall, they are excellent resources for learning how to manage your money and plan for your financial future. Personally, Suze is my favorite. When I was in college, I had terrible credit and no clue how to fix it. A few Google searches later, I found Suze Orman and learned how to fix my credit myself from her credit kit. I have followed her over the years and have always found her advice relatable and actionable.

RECLAIM YOUR EMOTIONS

There's more good news to counteract the effects of negative media. You recall the psychological "negativity bias" we discussed in Chapter Two, where we give more weight to negative information than positive? To counterbalance that, your brain has a built-in *physical* bad-news filter, called the "inferior frontal gyrus." This part of your brain generates an optimistic bias that pushes back against bad news. It allows us to believe that we could have avoided that traffic accident we just witnessed, or that we'll certainly live longer than that colleague who just died of a heart attack. Positive thinking may sound an awful lot like living in denial, but in fact the stronger your optimistic bias is, the healthier you are, mentally and physically.[60] Optimistic people spend less time researching their symptoms and illnesses online.[61] And optimists are more likely to practice positive health habits and therefore live longer.[62] Optimism, it seems, is a wonderful elixir.

You can nurture your inferior frontal gyrus by practicing

optimism with things like gratitude journaling, random (or scheduled) acts of kindness, and meditating on the kind of person you'd like to become—your "best future self." Taking just five minutes to be thankful for the people in your life can make a huge difference. If you just hate people right now, maybe you could be thankful for your dog, or nature, or music. Whatever makes you happy, recognize it for five minutes a day.

These exercises don't just affect your personal feelings and your own life. They can affect everyone around you. Gratitude makes you more empathetic toward other people, and helps you see things from their point of view.[63] Optimistic people have larger social networks, and stronger support from their friends and their community.[64] **A regular practice of gratitude and optimism can heal your heart and maybe even help heal our divided society.**

THE REBOOT YOUR FEED CHALLENGE

If you completed the challenges for Chapters One and Two, you should already see a change in your relationship to online shopping and social media marketing. Let's extend that to your content consumption. This challenge is a little longer. Let's see if you can go for two weeks.

If your clicks build your world, let's make it a good one.

- **Day One:** Don't click on any bad news or negative news stories—no matter what. Even if it's just to gloat about bad things happening to terrible people. No. Bad. News. Maintain this commitment for the rest of the challenge.
- **Day Two:** Pick one newspaper you trust that you can receive at home,

by local delivery or by mail. Subscribe to the print version of the paper you chose. You can probably get a sweet introductory rate. Keep on policing your clicks—no bad news.

- **Day Three:** When your new subscription arrives, boycott online news altogether. If you want to read a different newspaper, visit a bookstore or newsstand (or go to the public library).

- **Day Four:** Start feeding the content algorithm nothing but common sense and positive thinking. If you search for financial education (or anything else), go out of your way to click reputable resources, and avoid anything with a "get rich quick" or "doom and gloom" vibe. The more positive options you click, the more winners the algorithms will supply.

- **Days Five through Thirteen:** Review your group memberships. Algorithms pay attention to your interests, so do these groups represent what you want to see in the world? If they are toxic or contentious, you should probably put them on mute or leave them altogether. Try running this simple test: does this group make you feel fired up toward some positive action—or just fired up, period? If you leave the conversation wanting to volunteer for local campaigns, donate funds toward hurricane relief, give blood, or knit beanies for preemies, that's a group worth sticking with.

- **Day Fourteen:** Check in with yourself. How do you feel? Was it easy or hard? Could you keep it up for the rest of the month? How about the rest of your life?

Optimistic as we may want to be, there is no way to sugarcoat it: the internet is a minefield of lies and misinformation. Too many entities are motivated to slant your thinking their way—especially when it comes to your finances. The sad fact is that whenever money is involved, you can't take anything at face value. It's time to educate yourself, polish up that shield of financial facts, think positively about your future, and become a conscious media consumer.

Armoring up will help you even more as we tackle our next topic: how brainhacking undermines our impulse control, and the dangers of having the whole world just a click away.

CHAPTER FOUR

THE WORLD AT OUR FINGERTIPS

We've spent a lot of time talking about history, society, and theory, and we have more in-depth information to cover about the science and data behind brainhacking. We need to come up for air! Let's change gears for a moment to look at the impact of brainhacking in real life, and some practical steps you can take right now to fight back.

I promised you true confessions, so let me tell you about the donut debacle of 2019.

One fateful night, I was craving donuts. To me, these little bites of fried pastry are absolute heaven—but I'm a bit picky. Either Krispy Kreme or a mom-and-pop shop, thank you very much. The problem was that Doordash didn't list any shops open within my delivery area. Disappointing—but maybe not surprising, considering that it was already the middle of the night. Not exactly prime donut-buying time.

I decided to plan ahead and Google somewhere to grab a dozen in the morning. My search returned only two options in my area: either this disgusting chain that became famous a few years ago when people posted videos of rats crawling all over their donuts—at the very same location I was seeing on Google (no joke), or this super trendy place that only sold flavors like sea-salt maple or peanut-butter-lavender for nine dollars each. Nine dollars! Not happening.

At this point, I started thinking, "Is there a hole in my local donut scene?" (Pun totally intended.) "If I opened up a Krispy Kreme, could I become a millionaire?" An hour later, I'd done all the math and decided Krispy Kreme would not pencil out. I was going to build my own shop from the ground up and launch a puffy, sugar-glazed empire. Of course, to achieve that, I'd need to learn to make donuts. And for that, I'd need supplies. It was now 2:00 a.m.

So I moved to the Williams-Sonoma site to see if they could fix my problem. Cart full, I realized their shipping would be way too slow—I was fired up *now* and couldn't wait until next week. Could I walk the ten blocks to the brick-and-mortar store for supplies in the morning? No—then I'd have to hire a car to haul it all home, and as a new business owner, I had to watch my startup costs.

By now it was three thirty in the morning. I had no supplies, no plan, and scant few hours before my real job started. I was starting to wonder if this whole donut-empress idea was so solid after all. But did I decide to go to bed, wake with fresh eyes, and walk through the neighborhood to see if donut shops were really in such short supply? Nope. I turned to my best friend for impulse buys, Amazon. Soon every donut-making supply in the Amazonian universe was winging its way to my house.

The morning it arrived, I was excited. Here we go, billion-dollar empire on the way! So it was time for one last search: "How to make the best donuts." I was going to compare recipes and alter the best ones to perfection. But three clicks later, I was reading that every oil used to fry donuts will give you cancer and kill you dead. A few more, and I was learning the top five signs that cancer is silently murdering you—and realizing I had every symptom listed.

By afternoon, my craving for donuts, some sleep-deprived decision-making, and the sheer simplicity of online ordering had landed me with $500 in donut equipment and a newfound certainty that I was dying of cancer. Three years later, I finally gave in and donated all that equipment to Goodwill. I never even opened the boxes.

I think we can all agree that what makes this country wonderful is the American dream—the idea that anyone can do or be anything. But my goodness, the American dream is deadly when it's 3:00 a.m., you're hungry, and your credit card information is prestored on Amazon. I could come up with this hare-brained dream at midnight and be on my way to my donut-queen coronation by morning.

Because here's the thing about online shopping. At this point in history, we have the entire world at our fingertips—and it's way too easy to hit "Buy Now." If I'd had to wait five days for Williams-Sonoma to deliver my donut machines, would I have checked out? No. If I'd had to walk down to their storefront, find each item individually, and carry them out with my actual hands? Not a chance. But I didn't have to wait. I didn't even have to enter my credit card information. All the usual opportunities for rethinking my choices had been stripped.

The internet removes every barrier standing between you and your most impulsive impulse buys. This is very much by design—and very much a direct threat to your financial security. So what's your job now? To slow down, pay attention, and start putting those barriers right back into place.

SLIPPING OUT OF CONTROL

Let's say you're sitting at your laptop, totally focused on work. Then suddenly, someone walks in with a piece of chocolate cake. A moment ago, you weren't hungry—food hadn't even crossed your mind. But now, well, you're not going to be rude, are you? They even brought you a fork. Of course you'll try a bite.

This is what getting online without barriers can look like. You might have no interest in cake (or shoes or French décor or hunting gear), but then there it is on your screen, delivered up as if on a serving platter. You might even be on a diet—or a budget—but if you don't have a plan for when this moment arises, you might not think twice about grabbing that fork.

The human brain is a unique organ because it tells itself what to do: pay attention, remember things, stay on task, control that impulse, decide what to do next. These instructions your brain gives itself are called "executive functions," and too much internet browsing weakens them. According to researchers at Ohio State University's Wexner Medical Center, the biggest victims are our attention span and short-term memory. Multi-tasking, such as when we're navigating the internet's various messages, pop-ups, and click-baited snares, hinders our ability to focus on a cognitive job. Because we're overwhelmed by all the distractions, we lose the ability to ignore them. Without focus and self-control, we lose sight of our own goals and become vulnerable to digital manipulation.[65]

(NOT SO) FUN FACT

Speaking of attention, researchers say that as the number of distractions in our lives has grown, our attention spans have decreased. In 2015, researchers in Canada did a survey of two thousand people and performed electroencephalograms on 112 volunteers. They found that the average attention span was eight seconds, a big drop from about twelve seconds in the year 2000.

Eight seconds. Goldfish have a longer attention span. Dory from *Finding Nemo* with her attention span of nine seconds is still doing better than the average person. The researchers attributed the decline in our focus to the heavy use of digital devices.[66]

One of the key points in BJ Fogg's *Tiny Habits* is a core principle of the tech world: sellers will do anything to reduce what Fogg calls "friction" and I call "barriers"—those little hiccups in the purchasing process that slow you down and let you reconsider your choices. If you can buy something in three easy clicks (or two, or one), your logical-processing faculties are far less engaged—you are literally less conscious of what you are doing. And an unconscious consumer is a valuable consumer.

Why do you suppose even brick-and-mortar retailers have moved so much of their business online? Think of the last time you went to a Target or Walmart. You saw some bare shelves, right? That's not wholly due to the supply-chain issues we've seen in recent years. It's because retailers know that human beings will default to the easiest choice, and we're far less likely to make rational decisions when click-click-clicking away at home, bored on the sofa.

Don't worry—you don't need to quit online shopping altogether. But you do need to start recognizing the spots where developers have smoothed out all that money-protecting friction. That way, you can start roughing up the path again with a few simple barriers.

BARRIER 1: DELETE STORED PAYMENT METHODS

Typing your shipping address and credit card number into a website every time you're going to make a purchase is annoying—which is exactly why you should do it. Think of it this way. If taking the extra two minutes to find your wallet and to enter your payment info is enough to make the purchase not worth your time, then *you do not need this item*. You just don't. What could be a simpler barrier to unconscious, irrational buying than that?

So right now, get onto all your favorites—Amazon, Facebook, Apple, whatever sites you frequent—and delete the information for your credit cards, as well as any other payment services you use, such as Venmo or PayPal. Make no exceptions, or you're setting yourself up for failure. Want to know how I know that? A couple years ago I decided I needed to quit shopping online.

(The donut debacle might have had something to do with this.) So I removed my stored payment data for all methods except PayPal, since I hated PayPal and only used it a couple times a year. Fast-forward to today, and you know what I use on every purchase to avoid having to get out my wallet? Yep, PayPal. So make sure you clear them all.

By the way, if you find yourself asking, "What about 'buy now, pay later' services like Klarna?" then it's time to put down this book and slap yourself across the face. I'm serious—a good hard smack.

Wow, this book just got violent. I did warn you there would be scary moments.

Seriously, if all my years in lending have taught me anything, it's that any service that breaks payments into installments is only breaking your future into pieces. Other than a house, car, or education, if you cannot afford to buy something outright, do not buy it. End of story.

BARRIER 2: SET UP UNBREAKABLE RULES

In 2021, I was bitten by a bat. Was I exploring some dark cave at night? On an exotic trip in the rainforest? Nope—just opening a patio umbrella. In 106-degree weather. At noon. In sunny California. (Did you know bats hide in umbrellas? Shake that thing before you open it. I may have just saved your life.)

The whole experience was quite bizarre, but I ended up feeling inspired by this little bat. As I lay in bed recovering from the required rabies shots over the next few weeks, I began hunting down the best in bat-themed Halloween décor. However—with the donut debacle still lingering in my mind—I decided to put a certain safeguard on my shopping choices. Every time I filled my cart, I had to wait twenty-four hours before buying. If I changed the cart at all, I would have to wait another twenty-four hours. This forced me to consider which items I actually wanted. I felt quite proud of my restraint.

Then in mid-October, I began to wonder when all these wonderful decorations were going to show up. So I opened up my emails and credit card histories to find that, lo and behold, I'd never actually completed the purchase. After spending hours researching and selecting each perfect item, I hadn't pulled the trigger. You know what that told me? That none of it was all that fabulous after all.

Instead of doing what I would have in 2019—that is, having the whole order overnighted to me ASAP—I decorated using what I already had in the house. And you know what? It looked amazing. In all my focus on finding exactly the right bats, webs, and spiders, I'd forgotten what I already had lurking in my basement: boxes upon boxes of bats, webs, and spiders. Money saved: $350.

In addition to the twenty-four-hour rule, my two most helpful personal rules are *never pay for shipping* and, as I mentioned in Chapter Two, *never click on an ad*. Those three rules together create just enough friction to make you stop and think. When you do, in all likelihood, you'll realize you don't need that item after all.

BARRIER 3: KEEP A MONEY JOURNAL

This barrier is all about personal accountability—and of course, about making online shopping just a bit less easy and a bit more irritating. Buy yourself a physical, paper journal—not off Amazon—or print my free template from www.jenniferbeeston. com. Now every time you want to buy something online, you have to record these details:

1. What item did you buy, and on what date did you buy it?
2. How much did it cost?
3. What time of day was it when you made the purchase?
4. Why did you decide to buy it then?
5. How did you feel when you made the purchase? (Especially note whether you were bored, exhausted, angry, or sad.)
6. How did you feel when the item arrived?
7. Did you know what was in the package before you opened it?

Writing all this out should have three major effects on your spending habits. First, let's be honest—you want to avoid this even more than you want to avoid repeatedly inputting your credit card info. That makes it an instant barrier to impulse buys. Second, tracking your purchases will force you to justify them, examining the thought process behind each one. Did you actually need a new set of matching corkscrews, or was your phone screen just the most interesting thing in the room? And third, keeping a money journal should help you recognize patterns in your own behavior. Are you most prone to buying at a certain time of day or when you're in a particular mood? The algorithms already know these details about you—so there's no sense keeping yourself in the dark.

BARRIER 4: CUT THE CORD

Journaling will help highlight unhealthy patterns in your buying. So now that you've recognized these patterns, let's put them to work—by cutting the cord during your most vulnerable moments. It might be that you're most susceptible to spending in the middle of the workday when you're stressed or anxious, or at ten o'clock at night if you're bored or lonely. Figure out what time you're most exhausted or vulnerable and mark it as "no-tech time" in your calendar. That's because making decisions is mental work, and the more tired we are, the worse we get at it.

Studies show that the more decisions you make in a day, the harder it is to regulate your impulses.[67] One 2007 Cornell study found that we make 226.7 decisions each day just about food, never mind the rest of our lives.[68] Observations of elementary-school teachers found that they made an average of 1,200 to 1,500 judgment calls each day during student interactions.[69]

Decision fatigue can have real and far-reaching effects. For example, a study by Princeton economist Dean Spears found that when poor people shop, they are more likely to snack during the shopping trip than a rich person. The explanation seemed to be that poor people have to do far more calculations about what to buy on their limited budget, so that by the time they reach the check stand they are mentally exhausted and don't have the willpower to resist impulse buys.[70]

Personally, I've realized that I make my worst decisions after work. I'm guessing this is pretty common. In the morning, we might be all "yoga, then an egg white omelet with broccoli," but we all know that by evening it's a candy bar and a bag of kettle chips.

In any case, my job tends to require long hours, so all I want to do with my evenings is unwind. For years, I followed the same pattern: by seven at night, I'd be sprawled across the sofa next to my husband, dog on my lap, TV blaring in the background as I scrolled through Instagram, TikTok, and various shopping sites. My attention was about as split as it could be—I wasn't fully engaged with my husband, dog, the show we were watching, or anything I was doing online. These were prime unconscious-consumption conditions, and my bank account was feeling the pain.

After I recognized this pattern, I created a new one: every night after work, I turned off my phone. I went for a walk, read a book, actually talked to my husband...and you know what? Not only did my spending come swiftly under control, but I also felt less pressure and anxiety overall. For such a simple barrier, it did me worlds of good.

In fact, the sooner you get away from tech at night, the better. Your sleeping and waking cycles are governed by light exposure, and dim light after the sun goes down causes the pineal gland in your brain to secrete melatonin. Blue light (like the light from phone and computer screens) mimics bright early-morning sunlight, making you more alert. This unnatural exposure disrupts your melatonin response much more than other colors of light.[71] So, when you lie in bed scrolling your newsfeed, the blue light wakes your brain up instead of calming it down, and if the content is stressful or engaging, that makes it even harder to relax and fall asleep.[72]

"Our evening texting, television shows, or video games are stimulating in themselves, keeping the brain busy and wound up, and even causing adrenaline rushes instead of calm," says Dr. Joanna Cooper, a neurologist and sleep medicine specialist in the Bay Area.[73]

Now, you try it. Come on—just for a week or two. Is there really anything that pressing on Facebook or Instagram that you're going to miss out on? Is there really anything on Amazon that you need to buy? You've identified the hours when you're most vulnerable to the algorithm beasts stalking you online. So when that time comes, just do yourself a favor and get out of the hunting grounds.

Feeling hesitant? If you're like many people, turning off your phone might make you nervous—after all, what if there's an emergency? I've got a pretty good workaround for that. In addition to my smartphone, I have a twenty-dollars-per-month "dumb" phone with no apps and no connection to any of my accounts. My family has the number in case of emergencies, and I can make outgoing calls if I need to. Problem solved. Meanwhile, if you find yourself suddenly thinking of a purchase you "need" to make right away, write it on a piece of paper and check it in the morning. I guarantee that purchase will look a lot less important by then.

In addition to noticing your vulnerable times of day or states of emotion, watch your money journal for recurring types of unnecessary buying. My friends on Instagram have pointed out my tendency to buy any stupid piece of fitness equipment that shows up on Instagram. I'd like to pretend they're wrong—but then I remember the piece that's supposed to make squatting easier. Squatting! An exercise that requires nothing but the ground beneath your feet.

At this point, I've taken to screenshotting anything fitness related and posting it to my stories before I buy. If nothing else, it gives my friends plenty of opportunities to mock: "Oh God, Jennifer, not again!" "Oooh, can I have it when you're sick of it in a month?" That mockery usually does the trick to stop me from buying it.

What are your buying weaknesses? Highlight recurrent themes in your money journal so that when the impulse to boredom- or anxiety-shop hits, you'll have that little PA system ready to blare in the back of your head: "Not the fat ironer, Jen. It's not worth it."

BARRIER 5: CONSIDER BETTER WAYS TO USE YOUR MONEY

As we discussed in Chapter Three, financial education in the United States is a joke. In 90 percent of calls I have with first-time homebuyers, I have to explain how to create and maintain a budget. Fortunately for you, there are dozens of free, effective budgeting apps available, such as Mint. Choose one, input the necessary bank and credit card information, and set your financial goals. Then let those goals be your guide when considering whether your purchases make sense—or whether you want to put that money toward some better end.

Say you're really proud of finding a Pilates mat that perfectly matches your exercise bands. Will you still be proud when you check your budget and realize you're not maxing out your 401(k)? Let me give you a wake-up call: by most accounts, Americans are doing a terrible job saving for retirement. In one analysis by the Transamerica Center for Retirement studies, the median amount that people have set aside is $93,000. That's a great amount for someone in their twenties or early thirties, but it's woefully inadequate for almost anyone else. Most jobs don't have pensions, most don't have retirements, your 401(k) will probably be several hundred thousand dollars short of your actual needs, and Social Security will not be enough to support your current lifestyle. Saving for retirement might not give you that peppy "buying high" in the moment, but it will offer a lot more peace and joy in the long term.

Personally, I tend to overspend around the holidays, so keeping my long-term goals in mind has saved me on more than one occasion. A couple of Decembers ago, I was reviewing some of my Instagram traffic when an ad popped up. It was a pair of Nutcracker-themed Christmas pajamas, with the "Deez Nuts" meme. My teenager would think they were hilarious. It's vulgar and offensive, but the nineties have come back around. They were fifty dollars, but I want to be the cool mom who makes my teenager laugh!

So I clicked. Despite my never-click-on-an-ad rule, I did it anyway. I got all the way to the checkout, and they wanted to charge me eleven bucks for shipping. Oof. Hilarious those pajamas might be, but I still wasn't going to pay for shipping. Having multiple layers of rules created a safety net. I blew through the no-ads and the twenty-four-hour rules, but the no-shipping rule stopped me.

Once I stopped to think, I could clearly see that buying them didn't align with my financial goals. So instead of hitting buy, I clicked out of the website and invested fifty dollars in cryptocurrency on my son's behalf. He was thrilled. As much as he would have loved those pajamas, they would have ended up in the garbage in a couple of months, while that crypto has the possibility of growing—plus, I got to be the cool mom who knows about crypto.

Like me, you might be a sucker for the perfect holiday gift or decoration. But every dollar you spend is an investment in something. Why not choose a longer-term source of happiness, satisfaction, or peace of mind?

BARRIER 6: PICTURE THE IMPACT OF YOUR PURCHASES

Another approach to protecting your money is to frame your spending as a series of ethical choices. The supply shortages of 2021 highlighted that we Americans regularly consume to excess—and the bulk of that excess ends up in landfills. At this point, our country produces so much more trash than we can process that we actually pay to ship our garbage to other countries. This not only wastes our tax dollars but pollutes the world at large, specifically nations too small to address those pollutants.

Although some clean plastic recyclables are processed in the US, an estimated 80 percent of our mixed plastics are shipped abroad. China used to accept a lot of this waste, but in 2017 it stopped importing twenty-four categories of recyclable waste. Mountains of paper, plastic, and other materials piled up at recycling centers, and many cities and towns closed their recycling programs. Before long, the US began shipping waste to Malaysia and other Southeast Asian countries.[74]

But the recycling capacity in Malaysia, Vietnam, and Thailand were no match for China, and millions of tons of waste started piling up in those countries as well. Much of it wound up in unauthorized dumpsites in the jungle or outside poor neighborhoods.[75] A lot of it was dumped in the ocean.

These accumulating piles of garbage are only expected to get worse. According to *National Geographic*, half of the 7,800 million tons of plastic in the world was produced after 2004, and the World Bank predicts the amount of waste will grow another 70 percent over the next thirty years.[76] Before you click that Buy Now button, take a moment to envision the heaps of trash and clouds of smoke you're personally contributing to. Does your need for that extra yoga mat actually outweigh the global cost?

FUN FACT

If you think the "money as morals" approach might work for you, also take a look at the documentaries *The True Cost*[77] and *Trashed*.[78] Personally, I was stunned to see the effects of fast fashion on our ecology. Once you see the environmental damage fast fashion has done, it is hard to pick up a cute sweater in "this season's trend color." It isn't fun anymore—it just feels bad.

All those pretty dresses I wear on my YouTube channel come from Rent the Runway. By sharing and reusing clothing and accessories, this business model allows consumers to reduce the demand and production of new clothes, divert waste from the landfill, and create a more sustainable approach to fashion.

BARRIER 7: SLAM THE DOOR ON ADVERTISERS

A few decades ago, it wasn't uncommon for some plaid-clad salesman to show up at your door, case of goods in hand. Over time, these guys were replaced by phone solicitors, who were no less irritating: "Listen to me!" they all shouted. "You've never heard of this thing I'm selling, but you need it right now! Buy before you miss your chance!"

These days, we block spam callers and glare threateningly if door-to-door salesmen turn up on our stoops. But what many of us don't seem to realize is that we basically have those same salesmen in our kitchens, living rooms, and bedrooms twenty-four hours a day. Just a few weeks ago, Alexa interrupted my dinner to announce, "Jen, it's time for you to buy collagen creamer again." Instead of pounding on the door or jangling the phone off the hook, online sellers are bombarding us with advertisements, app notifications, marketing emails, and more, trying to trigger us to buy, buy, buy. Frankly, they don't deserve our attention any more than the door-to-door guys did. So for our final barrier of the chapter, let's talk about how to slam the door on advertisers before they can even start their pitches.

IGNORE ADS

Okay, yes, we've already talked about this rule. (And frankly, we will again.) But it bears repeating. Not only does refusing to click on ads prevent algorithms from learning what to feed you, it also prevents you from following those ads and making unnecessary purchases. Bonus, the less we click on ads, the less valuable they become to advertisers and hosts. Right now, retailers have every motivation in the world for manipulating our minds and wallets. Let's take those motivations away.

UNPLUG

Pull the plug on Alexa (or Google Home, or whatever "smart speaker" you may have). Think about when and why you use it. Do you really need to access those features all day, every day? These virtual assistants aren't really there to assist *you*. They are assisting marketers in extracting money from your wallet—and recording everything you say and do so they can target their advertising more closely.

UNSUBSCRIBE

Remember the research about how many decisions we make each day, and the more we make, the worse they get? Here's a scary thought: how much of your daily "budget" of decisions is being wasted on deciding what emails to delete?

If you're anything like most consumers, your inbox regularly fills up with emails trying to tempt you into visiting a seller's site. Thanks to the PPC algorithms, many of these emails are geared toward searches you've made in the past. Most also come with a time constraint: huge clearance sale, seventy-two hours only! And if my friends in the marketing world are right, these emails are also timed to drop into your account at the time of day when you'll be most likely to act on them. Essentially, they're little ticking time bombs of temptation.

You might be thinking, "Of course those emails are in there. I subscribed to them myself! I don't want to miss any sales." But here's my question: do you actually need what any of these advertisers are selling? Were you actually thinking, "My goodness, I could use some new sweatpants. If only a coupon would show up in my inbox?" Or are these advertisers actually luring you into "deals" that do nothing but waste your money? I guarantee that if you write down all the items you're currently looking for and buy nothing but those, you'll save hundreds more than you would by buying stuff you don't need on clearance.

Of course, the prospect of actually unsubscribing from each of your sellers probably sounds like a nightmare. I recently tried to sift through all seven thousand of my unread messages so I could unsubscribe as necessary—but after six hours of this, I'd barely made a dent (except in my forehead from banging it against the keyboard).

Here's a much cleaner way to fight these interlopers. Go to your inbox. Choose "select all." Then hit "delete." Yes, I'm suggesting that you delete everything in your inbox. Honestly, you can take the time to scroll back through the years and save anything special—but if it were really that important, wouldn't you have backed it up ages ago? No, the time has come to give yourself a fresh, unspoiled doorstep on which to mount your anti-salesman defense. From now on, every morning when you get up, unsubscribe from every retailer and newsletter that comes knocking at your metaphorical door.

What about legitimate news outlets? Kick them to the curb. Our goal here is to rid your world of as many triggers as we can, to make you as conscious and intentional about your spending as possible. If you want to read the news, choose a reputable outlet and, at a time of day when you're less emotionally vulnerable, visit their site of your own volition. But what about retailers you actually love? Every time you hesitate to unsubscribe from a particular seller, just remind yourself of this: their whole marketing strategy is designed to turn you into a reflexive, unconscious consumer. All these sales, coupons, and special offers are just poking at your comatose body and saying, "Hey. Hey you, down on the ground. Give me some money."

STOP

This is what you should reply to all the marketing texts you receive. You may have willingly handed over your phone number in order to get 10 percent off of a purchase, and been harassed with promotional spam texts ever since. Reply "unsubscribe" or "stop," and clear another level of tempting clutter right off your phone.

SLOW YOUR ROLL

My donut debacle might've been extreme, but I'm not the only person to have gone on an ill-conceived midnight spending spree. Online buying is simply too easy, quick, and pleasurable for our own good. Of course it is—it's designed that way. So don't be afraid to take a pause at every phase of your buying process, ground yourself in the choices you're making, and ask some serious questions. Does this purchase align with your long-term goals? Would this same money be better spent elsewhere? What are the ramifications—financial, ethical, ecological—of this buy? And most tellingly, did you seek out this purchase, or did it show up at your door unannounced, briefcase in hand?

We'll dive even further into questions like these in our next chapter as we explore just why advertisers are so good at deceiving us: the science behind brainhacking.

—————

CHAPTER FIVE

THE BIOLOGY OF BRAINHACKING

Misdirection.

Emotional triggers.

Distraction.

Lowered inhibitions.

We've seen *why* brainhacking exists, *what* it does to us as individuals and as a society, and we even took a step back to see some actions we can take to start defending ourselves. But to really know the enemy, we need to see exactly *how* it works. Take a deep breath, and come with me on our next deep dive into the biological "back doors" brainhackers are using to manipulate your mind.

THE ULTIMATE EARWORM

One of the scariest *Star Trek* storylines I've ever seen was in *Wrath of Khan*. Basically, a parasitic worm crawled into Chekov's ear, penetrated his skull, and allowed the vengeful, diabolical Khan to take over his brain. I saw it when I was about ten years old, and the prospect of being overtaken and mind-controlled by some egomaniacal dictator, losing my sense of self, was next-level terrifying for me. For a full year, I scoured my bedroom for worms and slept with earmuffs every night. Needless to say, my parents banned me from watching anything Trek!

Welcome to 2022, where mind control isn't done by space worms, but by the smartest tech developers, savviest market-ers, and most advanced artificial intelligence in the world. With every purchase you make, picture ten men, three women, and a battalion of robots poised around a boardroom table somewhere, debating your next move. They watch your searches and take note: "Oh, period pain. Looks like this one's menstruating—push the chocolate. And this guy just viewed constipation—better send him an ad for Miralax." They're scrolling through your Facebook photos, learning about your children's interests, tracking what other local moms and dads buy online. They're making deductions about your medical history, mental health, sexual orientation, relationship status, and more—all so they can manipulate you into handing over your money.

It's scary how accurate and effective this manipulation can be. So let's talk about the "wonder drug" of brainhacking: dopamine. We'll look at how it functions in your brain, how brainhackers use it to manipulate us, and how that manipulation affects our everyday lives.

WHAT'S THE DEAL WITH DOPAMINE?

As we discussed in Chapter One, dopamine is a chemical produced in the reward center of the brain. Dopamine allows us to feel pleasure, satisfaction, and motivation. It helps us stay focused, work hard, and find things fascinating.[79]

If you have low levels of dopamine, you might feel apathetic or lazy. Low levels can be caused by stress, insufficient sleep, drug abuse, obesity, or a diet high in sugar and saturated fat. In some people, the nerve cells that produce dopamine gradually die, leading to Parkinson's disease. Too much dopamine is also a bad thing; it can make you more competitive, impulsive, or aggressive.[80]

You might feel a surge of dopamine during a new romance, when you get triple clovers on a slot machine, during a drug high (don't do drugs, kids!), or when you get validation from your peers. This last one is so effective that every social media platform on the planet has been developed with the aim of getting you addicted to dopamine through notifications, likes, comments, and other forms of social validation. Every time you get a "hit" of dopamine, your brain wants to repeat the same action to get another reward. This is referred to as the "dopamine cycle": a pattern of motivation, reward, and reinforcement.

But that cycle doesn't stay the same over time. You can't just keep repeating the same actions to get the same "hit" forever. Let's say you have some lab rats who are used to the same bland, nutritionally balanced rat chow every day. One day, you give them some cheese, and their dopamine spikes—the unknown and new make a big impact on the reward center. Now the rats love the cheese and want more, more, more.

However, if you feed a rat nothing but cheese every day for a month, it's not new anymore. It's predictable and boring. That big dopamine surge at the beginning tapers off into a slow and inevitable shift downward over time. The only way to get that rat to have another dopamine response to food is to make it uncertain what food will come next—you have to mix up its menu so each meal is a surprise. This creates anticipation. Soon, the rat is craving cheese again.

Now, the rat isn't addicted to the cheese, per se. It's addicted to the anticipation: the mix of desire and uncertainty. Because this is addictive behavior, the longer the rat goes without receiving a treat, the more often and more intensely it will pursue one. If the treats stop coming altogether, this quest becomes more and more intense until eventually, the anticipation wears off and the cycle is broken. In order to keep the addiction going, those treats must be dispensed far enough apart that the rat feels the craving, but close enough together that it never gives up completely.

This is precisely what social media is designed to do to us: to feed us just enough predictability that we anticipate a "treat," and just enough variety that we don't know exactly when it will show up. Am I saying that when it comes to social media, you and I are lab rats? Yes. Yes, I am.

To escape that depressing thought for a moment, let's get out of the lab and into the glamorous and sexy world of Las Vegas, to take a deeper look at how dopamine affects our choices.

THE SLOT MACHINE EFFECT

Gambling releases dopamine. Not just winning—the process of gambling creates anticipation, and winning is the unpredictable reward that reinforces it. There is that brief period when the slot machine reels are spinning or when you're waiting for the black-jack dealer's next card, when you are focused and enthralled. That's dopamine at work. The problem for a lot of people is that the dopamine is released even if they ultimately lose, and that makes it hard for some gamblers to know when to quit. The dopamine release process grows stronger and increases in intensity as these behaviors become habits.

Did you ever notice how much floor space casinos devote to slot machines? You'll always find a scattering of card-game and roulette tables, but slot machines fill every available corner. And each has its own novelty to offer: "Darn, I just lost at the Monop-oly slot. Guess I should go try the Lady Luck machine..." That's why it's not uncommon to spot the same person slotting it up at the breakfast buffet as you notice at dinner.

Do you think that poor soul has any idea how much money they've already lost? Of course not. They've spent the last twelve hours trapped in a continuous dopamine cycle: winning big, then chasing that high for minutes or hours at a time, certain that the next rush is right around the corner.

This illustrates another insidious influence at work, and this one is psychological. The sunk-cost fallacy is a cognitive bias that most human beings are susceptible to. When we've invested time, energy, or money into something, we feel attached to it and are reluctant to give up. We feel that if we just keep trying, we're bound to win sooner or later, but if we walk away, all that investment was wasted. This fallacy traps people into bad jobs, terrible relationships, dud stock purchases, and never-ending, random games of chance.

From the casino's perspective, these little machines are the biggest money-makers on the floor. Why? Because while you might believe you're playing with luck, you're actually playing against a sophisticated mechanism designed to manipulate your brain. The casino industry knows from long practice just what proportion of wins will keep gamblers playing the longest, and generate the biggest profit. Those percentage margins are regulated, as is the fact that the outcome must always be random. It's the randomness that gets you. If you pay attention, you'll realize that social media works in much the same way.

SOCIAL MEDIA "SLOTS"

The way social media pulls our brains' levers is very similar to the way slot machines work. Our smartphones are a boundless supply of social stimuli and thus dopamine. According to Trevor Haynes, a research technician in the Department of Neurobiology at Harvard Medical School, social media sites like Facebook, Instagram, and Snapchat trigger the same "neural circuitry" as slot machines. Smartphones aren't necessarily addictive, but the fact that they keep us in constant contact with hundreds of friends and billions of potential acquaintances certainly is. Humans have evolved as social animals. We thrive on that connection. So every time we get a text message or a like on a social media post, we get a dose of dopamine.[81]

This explains a lot. It explains why the average adult spends up to four hours a day glued to their phones. It explains why you feel your phone vibrating in your pocket even when it's silent. We're only human and when we get rewarded for a certain behavior, we are motivated to repeat that behavior.

Social media platforms are constantly reinforcing this dopamine feedback loop. They *want* you glued to your screen. Remember, Facebook, Google, Microsoft, Amazon, and all their social media minions make *billions* through advertising, and the only way they get paid is if they can catch your eye, keep it, and compel you to tap, connect, and keep coming back for more.

When I first created a Facebook account, I put up some mundane photo and was shocked when sixty people liked it. "My God," I thought, "I didn't even know I had sixty friends." I suddenly felt accepted, cool, a little more important than I had the day before—not because anything of value had changed, but because humans crave validation from our peers.

Now, about a hundred years later, it takes exponentially more likes for me to feel anything but anxiety. "Oh God, only sixty people liked my stuff! Do I post too much? Too little? Was it stupid? Do they think I'm stupid? AM I STUPID?" Maybe this little internal monologue sounds familiar to you. Maybe you've even found yourself constantly checking a post to see if that little "like" counter has ticked up. If so, keep in mind that the creators of that social media platform are aiming for this exact response. And they're manipulating you in at least two major ways to get it: the timing of your notifications and the exposure of your post.

TIMING OF NOTIFICATIONS

The goal of any social media is to increase your engagement

with their platform so they can expose you to as many ads—and therefore potential income for themselves—as possible. But not every person engages with social media at the same rate or for the same reasons, so developers have realized they can max out your interest by manipulating the frequency of your notifications.

Let's say we've got two Facebook users, Lucy and Michelle. Lucy posts some photos of her recent trip to Hawaii and then checks back fifteen times an hour, trying to figure out why more people haven't responded. "Do they all hate me?" she wonders—and it's to Facebook's advantage to keep her wondering. Withholding Lucy's notifications gives her the impression that her Hawaii trip is garnering less attention than it really is. Even better, it delays Lucy's dopamine hit, makes her feel panicky and undervalued, and encourages her to engage with their site as often as possible. In Lucy's case, bundling her notifications will get Facebook their maximum return.

However, not everyone's like Lucy. Her friend Michelle also went on this Hawaii adventure, but she doesn't care if people react to her photos of luaus and poke bowls. In Michelle's case, it's to Facebook's benefit to feed her each notification individually, trying to wear her down until she's gained enough interest to come engage with their app. They're tossing out a trail of cheese trying to lure that lab rat back into the experiment.

That's why Facebook is constantly expanding the number of notifications you get. It used to be that you could see what your 150 friends were up to, but now you get updates from the groups you join, the events you attend, and the artists you like. It's crazy and it's constant. These tempting shots of dopamine are on your phone, your laptop, your watch, your automobile dashboard. It's why Instagram often withholds "likes" so it can deliver them en mass for a dopamine crescendo.

"This variable reward schedule takes advantage of our dopamine-driven desire for social validation," Haynes explained. "It optimizes the balance of negative and positive feedback signals until we've become habitual users."[82]

EXPOSURE OF POSTS

The second way developers control your dopamine drip is by manipulating how quickly or widely your post is shown to other users. Slot machines can't allow their users to either win or lose constantly—they'll lose interest. Likewise, social media sites can't allow you to experience success at every turn—they need you to invest more time and engagement before they'll deliver the same high.

What might this manipulation look like? Let's say your baby photos on Monday receive two hundred likes, but those you post Tuesday receive only ten. Has your baby suddenly gotten uglier? Well, maybe. But more likely, the algorithm is only showing your post to a handful of people. It won't matter what time you've posted or whether everyone in your network follows you—they might never see what you've put online, regardless.

Your goal is to get more likes, shares, or positive responses. The goal of the *algorithm*, on the other hand, is to draw as many clicks as possible. It doesn't matter whether those clicks come from a follower of yours or from you yourself, endlessly refreshing and wondering why no one cares about your adorable child. In this kind of scenario, your uncertainty naturally drops you into the "craving" half of your dopamine cycle, causing you to search harder and harder for your next hit. At this point, you might create a new post—just like a slot-machine user pulling that lever—and try your luck again. And again. All of this keeps you, as well as your friends and followers, at maximum engagement.

Facebook and Instagram love to pull us in with their promises of social interaction and community building. But at the end of the day, these are money-making organizations. As far as they're concerned, you exist to give them clicks—no matter how depressed or addicted this leaves you.

WHERE'S THE UPSIDE HERE?

At this point, you might be wondering why I choose to use social media myself if it's so toxic. Yes, I recognize the irony of a woman who's built her career on social media pointing out its many flaws. As I mentioned up front, I'm not recommending that you stop using social media altogether. It is still an unparalleled platform for two-way communication on a national or global scale. In Chapter Nine, I'll look at many of the ways online communications can be—and are—used in positive and helpful ways.

I want to raise your awareness and motivation to make important changes to your relationship with social media. First, that you use it with intention: know exactly why you are there and what you are trying to accomplish. Next, that you don't internalize it: don't become emotionally attached to it, or allow it to define you.

Want to use Instagram to establish a brand or boost a business?

Wonderful! But if you're using it to justify your own existence, to prove that you have intrinsic value, get out now. These platforms are only designed to make you feel good in the short term. In the long term, they're all about keeping you on the hook, even if that means pushing you to the dark side of our dopamine cycle time and again.

You might be saying, "Okay, okay! I get it. I'll turn off my notifications. I'll keep in mind that Facebook, TikTok, and the rest are designed to manipulate my dopamine release."

Great! But these aren't the only problems you need to learn to combat. Let's look at how dopamine manipulation literally rewires your brain—and therefore your longer-term behavior.

THE CULTURE OF NOW, NOW, NOW!

Remember my donut debacle of 2019? That was a direct result of me expecting instant gratification—being unwilling to wait even a week or two to launch my midnight-craving-inspired new business. Our constant quest for dopamine has created new neural pathways in our brains, ones that demand immediate satisfaction.

The human brain has four main dopamine "pathways" for delivering chemical messages (a.k.a. neurotransmitters) to various parts of the brain. Three of these pathways are considered the "reward pathways" that deliver the neurotransmitter dopamine, and all three become active when we anticipate or experience rewarding events. In this way, they reinforce the link between certain behaviors and the reward that follows. Over time, these links become stronger and the neurons in our brain respond to certain stimuli with increasing intensity.[83]

Positive social stimuli—be it laughing faces, praise or gratitude from our peers, or messages from loved ones—activate the same dopaminergic reward pathways as a hit of cocaine, although the intensity is less pronounced.

"(Silicon Valley programmers) are shaping the thoughts and feelings and actions of people," Tristan Harris, a former Google executive, told *60 Minutes* in 2017. "They are programming people....They want you to use it in particular ways and for long periods of time. Because that's how they make their money."[84]

And it's not always for pleasure. In the same episode, psychologist Larry Rosen of California State University Dominguez Hills explained that the brain generates cortisol when we're waiting to hear if someone retweeted us or "liked" us. Cortisol is the brain chemical that triggers our fight or flight response to danger. We become anxious, and the best way to relieve that tension is to check our phone.[85]

Now, how can these newly rewired neural pathways, teeming with cortisol-induced anxiety and urgent cravings for dopamine, reshape your working, social, and financial well-being?

DOPAMINE VS. YOUR WORK LIFE

There I was on my wedding day, my makeup artist painstakingly applying liquid liner, when my phone rang. The number belonged to a client friend of mine. "Good God," I thought, "there must be some huge emergency if he's calling today!" I brushed aside my makeup artist—getting a long swipe of liner across my forehead as I did so—then answered the call.

"Hey, Jennifer," my work buddy said. "Can we chat about refinancing my loan?"

"I'm about thirty minutes from walking down the aisle," I responded. Which, for the record, he already knew.

Later that night, I got back from my reception to find a snooty email from this "friend." He was disappointed with my lack of dedication and had decided to go with a lender who was willing to make herself more available. I'd worked with this guy for ten years.

Now, to be fair to this work associate, I spent my early thirties answering every call, text, and email the moment it pinged into my phone, certain this was the way to cultivate a lasting career. I taught this guy that bothering me on my wedding day was okay—because I believed this kind of all-access pass was needed to succeed in my competitive field. But why do we allow our coworkers and clients to expect our attention 24/7? And why do we, in turn, expect the same of our coworkers, hair stylists, dog walkers, and educators?

For some good insight into this domino effect, take a look at the book *Do Nothing: How to Break Away from Overworking, Overdoing, and Underliving* by Celeste Headlee.[86] In essence, her point is that since the Industrial Revolution, our society has been flooded with time-saving technologies, yet we have less free time than ever. This is because our devices enable us to be chained to our work, bosses, and clients—basically, other people's expectations—twenty-four hours a day.

THE ARMS RACE OF PRODUCTIVITY

Since the beginning of the Industrial Revolution, people have been promised that innovation and machinery—in short, technology—would make our lives richer, freer, and more relaxed. Never happened. In fact, the opposite has happened. As more and more technology has pushed its way into our lives and work, most of us feel we work harder and put in longer hours. But we rarely feel a sense of accomplishment because there is always *more we could be doing*. Life and work have become an endless scroll, a bottomless pit of empty promises.[87]

Isn't gonna happen. Even though we *do* have robots delivering meals to office buildings, electronic vacuums running while we're at work, and driverless cars to take us to and from our jobs, many of us are still drowning when it comes to workload. Our bosses always expect more and many of us, if the truth is told, get a little nervous when we take an afternoon off. Will we fall behind? Will everyone else get ahead? What if we miss an important announcement? For many people, working hard is their badge of commitment.

At the same time, screen use chips away at our productivity. We're constantly distracted by news alerts, social pings, emails, and text messages zipping into our inboxes. How many times have you been busy writing a report for work when your mind drifts to your next vacation, and suddenly you're checking plane fares on Expedia?

Most of us think we're working with great focus when we're enduring an ongoing series of interruptions, but according to the *Psychonomic Bulletin & Review*, we are not the highly skilled multitaskers we think we are.[88] Trying to do multiple things at once actually reduces our productivity. According to research from the University of California at Irvine, it takes over twenty-three minutes for most of us to return to a task after an interruption.[89]

What kind of damage does this cause? According to Professor Gloria Mark, who led the study at UC Irvine, all this distraction heightens stress. Mark studied two groups of office workers— one group assigned to answer a series of emails without any interruption, and a second group doing the same thing, only with a series of phone calls and instant messages. Those who were interrupted recorded higher stress levels, frustration, time pressure, and mental workload. Interestingly, the people who weren't interrupted worked more slowly. Those who were being interrupted tended to speed up to compensate.[90]

The speed of technology is always increasing, and we are always trying to keep pace. "While it can help us work faster, technology also makes us feel more pressed for time," says Dr. Aoife McLoughlin of James Cook University in Australia. "When the speed of the rhythm of life increases, the subjective feeling of having free or available time decreases, causing a feeling of stress within the individual."

The problem is that technology keeps us in constant communication with others. We get emails from coworkers at 2:00 a.m. and we *read* them because we're a) already wide awake *worrying about work* or b) we're glued to our phones flicking through our newsfeed in search of a dopamine-fueled sliver of reward.

"Although these tools were born as a source of autonomy and flexibility, in reality they intensify the expectations of constant communication and involvement at work, and consequently increase stress," explains Jorge Franganillo, researcher and professor of Information and Documentation at the University of Barcelona.[91]

During the 2020 pandemic, many companies shifted to remote and hybrid work. For many workers, four-day workweeks and reduced hours made them even more productive.[92] Studies have shown increased productivity when workers work from home, and more than a few people quit rather than return to their cubicles.[93] There's a growing feeling that "we have one life—and are we working to live, or are we living to work?" Rachel Deutsch, director of worker justice campaigns at the Center for Popular Democracy, told Vox in July 2021.[94]

In the Great Resignation of 2021, burnout was the number-one reason employees cited for leaving their jobs.[95] We can't ignore the effect of the pandemic, and how many of those burnt-out employees were in frontline fields where "burnout" is a nicer way of saying "trauma." However, a lack of work-life balance and the unrealistic expectations of hustle culture are important factors as well. In the same study I cited above, 64 percent of those resigning employees chose a new job with more flexibility.

However, remote, flexible work can be a Catch-22. One survey conducted after the COVID-19 pandemic revealed that about three in four professionals who worked from home also found themselves working longer hours and often on the weekend. They liked the flexibility of at-home work but found it difficult to disconnect from their work. They missed the natural boundary they crossed when they left the office at the end of the day.[96]

The personal impact of out-of-control work demands and burnout have morphed into broader social movements. While the eighties were all about chasing the corner office, the nineties celebrated "work hard, play hard," and the noughties glorified passion and fulfillment at work, Gen Z is leading a silent rebellion against the always-on work culture. In the US, the phenomenon of "quiet quitting" or work-to-rule is spreading through workplaces at every level. Instead of seeking "stretch goals" and aiming to impress, employees are doing only what is absolutely necessary under their job description. In China, the trend goes even further. Workers who join the "lying flat" movement (known as *tang ping*) deliberately do the bare minimum to avoid getting fired. This is a massive revolt in a system that celebrates "996," a shorthand for working from 9:00 a.m. to 9:00 p.m., six days a week. Some observers compare *tang ping* and quiet quitting to the hippie movement of the 1960s that urged overburdened young people to "tune in, turn on, and drop out."[97]

I have to say, I understand the sentiment. Burnout is real, and it's not sustainable for human beings to operate at the speed of tech. As a mortgage lender, I spend a good part of my time on non-client-facing work, like structuring files, dealing with underwriters, and managing my branch—but the always-on culture leads potential clients to find this unacceptable. In my industry, having a division between work hours and nonwork hours at all has become a radical concept. When I announced to my team that we were going to stop making ourselves available to clients on weekends (except in emergency cases), my staff reacted with fear. "We're going to lose our jobs!" they said. "We're going to hemorrhage clients!" My response? "Great. Then we'll just work with the clients who understand that we're not machines."

Concessions by employers, "permission" to work more sustainably, aren't enough. We must also have boundaries against overwork and tech-induced frenzy inside ourselves. And those are the exact type of boundaries that brainhacking is designed to blur.

So, what does all this have to do with unconscious spending? *Everything.* Look back at everything we discussed in the first five chapters, all the ways that tech is training your brain to crave more tech time, and spend more money: distraction, stress and anxiety, negativity and despair, eroded boundaries, lack of sleep, and impulsive choices. When you're always working, you aren't spending time taking care of your body, your home, and your relationships. You wait until a problem shows up, and then throw money at it. But that's not a healthy way to live, and it's not healthy for your personal relationships either.

INSTANT GRATIFICATION VS. YOUR PERSONAL LIFE

Once the always-on culture becomes a habit and you're chained to your tech, it becomes harder and harder to separate legitimate work tasks from the engineered pings and demands of our own personal brain-eating space worms. That constant distraction negatively impacts our relationships with loved ones. Social media can make us *feel* more connected, at least in the short term. According to the Pew Research Center, many teens believe social media helps them share an emotional connection with friends and significant others. They feel better knowing what's happening in their friends' daily lives and find it easier to share their true feelings. They may also experience feelings of jealousy or doubt. Either way, whether they experience good or unpleasant feelings, teens tend to feel that the impact of social media on their relationships is relatively benign.[98]

Couples forced to spend time away from each other also find that social media brings them closer to their partners.[99] And according to one article in *Psychology Today*, social media can also help partners show they care for each other. Gwendolyn Seidman, PhD, the author of that article, said her Facebook feed makes her husband's coworkers feel like they know her and makes them more comfortable in physical social settings.[100]

But the danger to relationships seems to be far more significant than the benefits. For instance, the time you spend glued to your screen is time you *aren't* spending in meaningful discussions or activities with your partner or children, and that can send the message that social media is more interesting than the people you love. I don't know about you, but I might never forgive myself for the number of times I uttered these words as a young mother: "Just a second. Mommy's got a text."

And since people tend to share their "best lives" on social media, spending a lot of time on Facebook or Instagram can make you feel like your own life is dull and unrewarding. "Wow. Bob and Cindy really are in love. Look, they're on a cruise! Now they're staying in a cute seaside bungalow. He's...cooking her a champagne brunch. I never get champagne brunches!" This can lead you to feel discouraged about your own relationship. Some research indicates that increased use of social media can predict a negative outcome for romantic relationships, including cheating, breakup, and divorce.[101] A thesis dissertation by Brigham Young University in 2018 found that social media overload diminishes your emotional wellness and lowers your satisfaction in your interpersonal relationships.[102]

Naturally, the pressure to remain constantly connected doesn't just affect people who are married or have children. What if you're trying to find love in this *Now-Now-Now* environment? A frustrated friend recently said to me, "Oh no, Jen. This guy I like isn't texting me back." I asked her how long she'd been waiting. "Ten minutes!" she moaned. "He usually responds in three!" She spent the next quarter hour stressing aloud: "Do you think my last joke was too forward? Did I screw this up? What if he's losing interest? What if he's—"

"What if he's in the bathroom?" I finally interrupted. "You really want him to text you on the toilet?" At this point, we as people are behaving more and more like computers when it comes to social situations—watching others' behaviors and making narrow, quick determinations about their motivations. Again, this is all because we've allowed dopamine-fueled media to train our brains for instant gratification.

Complicating the matter, as we saw with our lab rats above, a dopamine-addicted brain must constantly seek new forms of stimulation to achieve the same—or even a greatly reduced— hormonal high. This is similar to the effect of pornography addiction on the brain. Recent studies have shown a link between excessive or compulsive use of porn and the increase in erectile dysfunction in young men.

In a study at the University of Antwerp in Belgium, the more men watched porn, the more likely they were to have erectile dysfunction. In that study, 30 percent of the men under thirty-five who watched five hours of porn a week had problems getting and keeping an erection while only 10 percent of those who watched only a half-hour of porn a week had problems. About half of those with erectile dysfunction during partnered sex had no trouble rising to the occasion while watching porn.[103]

Pornography is all about instant gratification, about overstepping the usual expectations of social interaction to jump straight to the sex. It's instantly available everywhere, and much of it is free. But there's no way that real life can compete with the ease and fantasy of pornography, and many porn users have to chase ever-crazier sexual depictions to achieve the same high. As a result, many have difficulty performing sexually in the real world, since nothing real can stimulate them to the same degree.

In a similar way, an overdose of online distraction disconnects us from real relationships. I recently had to tell my husband, "You know, I'm never going to be as interesting as BringATrailer. com." Because, sorry, I'm not. At this point in history, we have to actively choose between chasing dopamine on games, news, or media, and cultivating closeness with actual people.

So then we're in an even more vicious cycle: the craving for dopamine makes us seek it. Real social connection and validation supply dopamine, but they are slow, complicated, and inconvenient, so we turn to our easy online sources. That immersion in a virtual online life distances us from real relationships in the real world. Our isolation from real relationships leaves us feeling empty, and at higher risk of depression and anxiety. As we discussed in Chapter Two, depression and anxiety make us more vulnerable to manipulative clickbait. So we crave those clicky-clicky dopamine hits all the more.

So where does all this lead us? Right back where we started: your finances.

INSTANT GRATIFICATION VS. YOUR WALLET

Chapter Four was all about instant gratification driving impulse purchases. But dopamine-fueled decision-making can have much more far-reaching implications than a random shopping spree. Here's the truth: if you're constantly seeking new stimuli, you're training yourself not to reflect on your actions before taking them. You're keeping yourself in a state of hormonal high alert. And although you should never—ever—make important financial decisions in fight-or-flight mode, some marketers are out to force you into doing exactly that.

Take one worrying trend in my own field: the "sixty-second" mortgage approval. Online lenders claim to approve you for a mortgage in anywhere from one to three minutes. *This claim is complete nonsense.* Any "approval" you receive will be based on data you input yourself, and will be subject to review by an actual lender. Because the average consumer makes errors while filling out the application, more often than not, that "approval" is either overturned or modified after review.

Here's how it works. You see an ad—"Qualify in under a minute!"—and decide to fill out an application. You're a smart and prepared applicant, but you still miscalculate, for example, your household income. Again, this is pretty typical. Many people work an hourly—not salaried—position, and most overestimate their average hours worked per week. You might also be unable to remember details about your property taxes, insurance, work bonuses, or HOA dues, any of which can affect your preapproval.

At this point, the website taking your information generates a quote based on your (possibly incorrect) data and spits out the good news: you're qualified, and for some spectacularly low rate! But the moment your info is reviewed by an actual lender, any mistakes you've made will push that rate up, up, up—or overturn your preapproval altogether.

By this point in the process, lenders have already sold you their fake bill of sale—the idea that they can fully approve you within a minute when in reality, *no one can*. But here's where this practice goes from misleading to actively sleazy: lenders know that you, as a consumer, have been trained to expect instant results—instant gratification. Remember the sunk-cost fallacy that helps make slot machines so hard to walk away from? Lenders are banking on it here too. They know that after you've gone to the effort of applying with them, you're less likely to choose a different lender—so you will accept whatever quote they offer, good or bad.

And they're not wrong to assume this. In 2019, a J.D. Power study found that record levels of credit card debt and rising interest rates had made personal loans the fastest-growing category of consumer debt products. Consumers particularly love being able to apply online; they are more satisfied with the loan they get and they believe the process is easier to understand. And when they can get a home equity line of credit in two days instead of the former average of twenty-six days, their customer-satisfaction ratings go through the roof. Nearly half of the borrowers choosing the fast and easy digital route also considered competing products.[104] In another study by Price-waterhouseCoopers, most consumers prefer online loans and believe the most important factor in choosing a lender is the speed of the process.[105]

That trend is frightening enough, but there are certain segments of the economy where "fast and easy" is a recipe for disaster. Frankly, if you're going to invest hundreds of thousands of dollars into a home, the implications of that decision should be explained to you at a level you can actually understand. You might be smart, prepared, and capable—but you're not an expert, and misleading lenders will do whatever they can to exploit that.

(NOT SO) FUN FACT

When your house payment eats up so much of your take-home pay that you can barely afford it along with your other living expenses and normal spending patterns, you are "house poor." It's a bad situation that can force people into tough choices like whether they will sacrifice cable internet or phone service (especially when they need both for their job). Or worse yet, whether they can pay for food and water. Sketchy lenders who approve too much, too quickly and don't look at a consumer's whole financial picture can and do put people in this position if they aren't checked.

In case it's not clear, I hate this practice. Despise it. Wish I could club it over the head with a tire iron. But ironically, the minute-mortgage claim has forced more traditional, education-first lenders like me to change our business approaches just to compete. I spend a great deal of my time on YouTube explaining how lenders look at income, how the preapproval process really works, and why it takes longer than a minute in real life. Speed is important—it's critical to my business—but that speed comes into play *after* you are in contract on a house. Once you are fully preapproved by my team and by underwriting, and once you are properly educated, then I can move like lightning. But not until we know that the loan product is right for you. Never, ever would I try to prey on you by selling you a lie, or setting you up to be house poor.

The PPC-driven, dopamine-fueled internet is picking money from our pockets by teaching us that no decision is worth making if it can't be made fast. Reject this idea. Slow down. Ignore the lure of instant gratification, of that dopamine high. Your financial future is worth the extra few hours, days, or even weeks of careful education, research, and choice.

UNHACK YOURSELF

In this chapter, we covered how developers and marketers try to hack your brain's biology. Let's consider a few final ways you can combat unconscious spending by getting off the dopamine-go-round:

1. **Turn off all your notifications—and I do mean *all*.** This will help you unload the ball and chain that Now, Now, Now! culture has strapped to your leg. Designate a time of day (e.g., five minutes at the beginning of each hour) to check your texts and emails, and refuse to step outside those selected times. If you have an Apple phone, use focus mode. I use mine constantly, and the clarity I get from not being constantly interrupted by calls and texts is priceless.

2. **Go onto social media only with intent.** Each time you're tempted to tap that icon, ask yourself why. "I'm lonely," "I'm sad," or "I'm bored" are not legitimate excuses—and if you're truly lonely or depressed, social media can only offer a temporary Band-Aid to your problem. We've covered how addictive dopamine is, so if you're just looking for a "hit," stop. Step away from the phone. The first step in breaking an

addiction is stopping. Remember, human beings are social creatures—we might not all be extroverts, but we all crave the attention, approval, and presence of our fellow humans to some degree. Social media can only offer the illusion that you're surrounded by friends. Participating in community events, volunteering, or taking a friend to lunch can fulfill your evolutionary need for company on a much deeper and more fulfilling level.

3. **Do not gauge your worth by social media's attention.** Likes and comments are just tools created by savvy developers to keep you coming back to their platforms. If your chosen platform offers the option, opt out of displaying your likes on the screen. It can only reduce your dependence on dopamine hits and improve your mental health.

When I was ten years old, Khan's evil mind-worms were the scariest things I could imagine. These days, I realize that brain-hacking is a real and constant threat, one that marketers and developers have down to a literal science. Never forget that marketers' primary goal is to lower your ability to say no—to make you an unconscious consumer.

But as devious and effective as advertisers can be, it's important to remember that we can fight them. The more you learn about their methods, the easier it becomes to spot them in action—and shake them off. They want you to be unconscious? Embrace consciousness! Find satisfaction in making each online choice with intention, eyes wide open.

The next major method we need to examine is the targeted personal surveillance marketers use to track our behavior and understand us better than we understand ourselves. They're peeking inside the human brain to pinpoint how we'll react to certain stimuli, and using our personal data to focus those stimuli to a staggering degree. Together, these techniques are known as "neuromarketing."

CHAPTER SIX

NEUROMARKETING

All the psychological and biological brainhacks in the world wouldn't work very well without inside information. And I mean *literally* inside—observing the behavior of the human brain in real time.

A few years ago, the Frito-Lay company invited a group of consumers to review a commercial spot in which a woman got revenge on a jerk at the laundromat by throwing Cheetos into the dryer with his white sheets. When asked for their thoughts and reactions, most people in the group responded with variations on, "Oh, that's not nice," "No, she shouldn't have done that," or "That's not good."

However, when the testers strapped each participant into an EEG, they were able to observe the areas of the brain that respond to engagement or emotional arousal. It was like hooking them all up to an unbeatable lie detector. When participants watched the ad again, they couldn't hide the truth: nearly all found the woman's actions hilarious. They'd never say that out loud, because they didn't want to sound like vengeful sociopaths.

The researchers found a way to circumvent their social filters and tap into their hidden responses.[106]

This is neuromarketing: the methods advertisers use to bypass what we claim to like or dislike to see what our brains actually respond to. Neuromarketing utilizes brain imaging, electroencephalography and eye and facial tracking systems to find out why people do what they do and not what they say they will do.[107] Marketers can use this information to find customers and craft ads that will work on them.[108] Done right, neuromarketing can pinpoint the precise moment when an advertiser's message is being most effective or when the consumer is growing distracted and disinterested.

Marketers are great at pushing our buttons, but they need to know exactly which buttons to push. In this chapter, we'll examine:

- the development of neuromarketing and hypertargeted advertising,
- the business of data brokering, and
- the dangers we face from constant commercial surveillance.

BETTER THAN YOU KNOW YOURSELF

Brand managers are always looking for insights into how their customers think and behave. Why do they buy one product over another, and what is the likelihood that they will buy it again? It seems like the simple answer would be to *ask* consumers about their shopping habits, but the truth is that consumers don't really know. They say one thing and do another. For example, they may tell you that they buy certain products because they're environmentally safe and align with their personal ideals, but when they start filling their shopping carts, environmental issues go out the window.[109] According to Will Leach, the author of *Marketing to Mindstates*,[110] "When it comes to buying decisions, most consumers are simply not thinking at all."[111]

But with neuromarketing, marketers can bypass consumers' biases and their unreliable explanations for their actions. Instead, marketers can monitor physiological and neural signals to learn about consumers' preferences, motivations, and decisions.

Sound a bit futuristic? Applying brain science to marketing was first studied in the 1990s. The term "neuromarketing" was coined in 2002 by a Dutch researcher at Rotterdam University. It went mainstream in 2004 in a high-tech version of the Pepsi Challenge, with blind taste testers strapped into a functional MRI. The researchers found that when study participants were given unlabeled samples of Coke and Pepsi, they favored Pepsi. When people drank the Pepsi blindly, their brains lit up as their reward systems became active. But when study subjects were aware of the brand of cola, they favored Coke. Their brains lit up in different areas associated with memory and emotion.[112] Pepsi tasted better, but Coke had better advertising.

Now, less than twenty years later, scanning consumers' brains with an EEG or MRI is about as commonplace as traditional consumer-response groups. Using this method, Frito-Lay has tested not just ads but also packaging, product design, and more. Pleasure, security, frustration, distrust: you name the emotion, marketers can find it in the brain. Neuromarketing confirms that people really do respond to images of babies, puppies, and attractive women. If you want your pet food to sell, make sure the print ad includes an athletic lady or chubby infant smiling at the can so consumers know just where to look.

It's effective. But is it ethical? Most of us like to believe that our innermost thoughts and feelings are private. Are we comfortable with this much interference in our subconscious minds? If we're not even aware of what's happening, how will we know if we're being hacked by a nefarious salesforce? Is exploiting our brains to keep us addicted to technology or products ethically any different from tobacco companies making their products more addictive?[113]

To be clear, I don't actually consider neuromarketing itself to be unethical. We can't expect marketers to advertise their products blind, and consumer-response groups are demonstrably unreliable. But never forget that advertisers' goal here is to appeal so directly to your brain's unconscious responses that your impulse control is reduced to a minimum. In the 2011 BBC documentary *Secrets of the Superbrands*,[114] neurologists found that when they hooked Apple fans up to an fMRI, their brains responded to the brand the same way that a religious person's brain reacts to the concept of God. These marketers don't just want your approval. They are seeking utter devotion and evangelistic fervor.

When you combine neuromarketing with hypertargeted advertising, you might as well open up your wallet and hand it to the advertiser.

HYPERTARGETING

Ordinary advertising uses broad-based research about socioeconomic or demographic groups to design ads and place them in the best possible context. Hypertargeted ads don't rely on the same kind of large-scale assumptions because they have the Holy Grail of market research: personal consumer data.

In 2012, the *New York Times* published a disturbing anecdote: a teenage girl received Target coupons for diapers, wipes, and baby bottles. Based on this girl's recent purchases—prenatal vitamins and a large purse that could double as a diaper bag—Target had correctly deduced that she was pregnant. Her father had no idea until he opened up the mailbox that day. His first response was to chew out the local store manager for being inappropriate. Later, he and his daughter had an important (and possibly overdue) conversation.[115]

I have an even scarier story. When one of my team members, Tegan, was a newlywed, she suddenly began seeing baby-themed posts on her Instagram feed. Baby-related profiles, ads for baby products, her whole Instagram was all about babies.

I told her, "Instagram knows. Go take a pregnancy test."

She didn't believe me at first, but lo and behold—the test came back positive. She hadn't searched for or clicked on anything related to babies. She had no idea she was pregnant. But Instagram had access to all the data on her phone, including the data from her period-tracking app. She hadn't looked at it in a while, so she didn't realize she was late. Instagram did.

We live in a surveillance nation. Collecting and trading in consumer data is a billion-dollar industry with limited oversight. Websites use an arsenal of tools to track your online activity, and the number is always increasing. Cookies are the most common way websites watch your activities. How many times recently have you clicked "I accept all cookies" when using a website? Do you even know what a cookie is?

FUN FACT

Cookies are small pieces of text saved to your browser by websites. There are two types of cookies used by the sites you browse online. **First-party cookies** belong to the actual site you're viewing. They help the site "remember" you, like keeping track of which articles you've read, or storing your login information. **Third-party cookies** (also known as tracking cookies) come from sites you didn't choose to visit (yet). They track your activity as you browse. They allow marketers to send customized ads to you, wherever you are. You know how those cool headphones you looked at seem to follow you everywhere? You're not paranoid. They are, in fact, following you like a burr stuck to your socks. More than 80 percent of web traffic contains third-party cookies.[116]

As of this writing, third-party cookies seem to be on the way out. The General Data Protection Regulation (GDPR) in Europe and the California Consumer Privacy Act (CCPA) in the US have caused Safari (by Apple) and Firefox browsers to disable third-party cookies. Google Chrome is set to get rid of third-party cookies in 2023. These changes are causing major shifts (and a good bit of panic) in the world of marketing, but since Google already moved its original target date back a year, we'll wait and see how these changes will play out.[117]

No matter how the cookie crumbles, they are just one tool marketers use to track and target you. Sites also use web beacons to see what content you click on, session replay scripts to record your mouse movements, clicks, and scrolls, and even "favicons," which are "supercookies" that are harder to detect or get rid of. Cross-device tracking lets advertisers see what you're doing on your desktop, laptop, tablet, and phone. By one account, Google tracks 80 percent of all web traffic, while Facebook tracks 20 percent and Amazon tracks 17 percent or so.[118]

What's the point of all this detective work? Money, of course. You don't make $200 billion a year on advertising, like Google does, if you aren't putting the ads in front of the customers most likely to buy. And don't think it's just search engines and social media sites that are watching you. As more people turn to streaming as their primary way of watching TV shows, streaming platforms are also aggressively getting to know you, so ad-supported channels can deliver the right digital commercials to your set. The fifty something neighbors in one apartment might be watching the same show as the twentysomething neighbor in the other, but they'll be seeing different commercials.

The bottom line is that advertisers can and will use your consumer data to manipulate you out of your money. Again, their goal is to lower your impulse control to its barest minimum. They've already learned to stimulate your brain with dopamine hits and emotional triggers. But now they're going to take their attacks to the next level by tracking your data, learning your precise pain points, and delivering neuromarketing-inspired advertisements tailored to you.

I find all this spying to be creepy. But even creepier is the fact that consumers seem to be increasingly comfortable with this

Big Brother BS. One study found that 43 percent of consumers agree it's "important" that ads are personalized, and 32 percent said they like the ads. Thirty percent of consumers say they like brands *more* when they personalize ads.[119]

I can only imagine that's because they don't understand the risks involved in online data collection. So let's get educated on that front, by talking about who's collecting and selling your data, how advertisers use that data to infiltrate your brain and compromise your personal and financial life, and what you can do to stop it.

DATA BROKERING

Data brokering is an entire industry of its own, with estimated revenue in the hundreds of millions of dollars. Once upon a time in the 1970s, fee-based information services were a rising business model, dealing with phone numbers, zip codes, and credit scores, usually from public data. By the 1990s, databases could contain a variety of personal information about voting preferences, court records, and bank card transactions—and calls for regulation arose. The amount and specificity of personal data collected has skyrocketed since then, but regulations continue to lag behind industry practices and technological ability.

Today, there are over 120 data broker firms in the US who are collecting and selling information about us. It's a murky corner of the economy, and the only reason we know about these firms at all is because Vermont passed a law in 2019 that requires third-party sellers to register with the state. First-party data brokers—outfits like Google, Facebook, and Apple, who collect mountains of data about their own users—aren't included.[120]

But the list nevertheless has some pretty big names on it, including Oracle, Acxiom, Spokeo, ZoomInfo, White Pages, PeopleSmart, Intelius, PeopleFinders, Equifax, Experia, and TransUnion. These firms are extremely profitable. For example, Acxiom, which owns data on 2.5 billion consumers in sixty-two countries, was purchased by an ad agency in 2019 for $2.3 billion. In 2021, the consumer data industry overall was valued at just over $1 billion and is growing annually by about 20 percent.[121]

We all know our data is being collected and sold by the sites where we shop, browse, and read, because we keep clicking on those "I accept all cookies" messages. But the rot goes much deeper than random commercial sites.

You might assume your credit card company would have your financial back, but don't assume too much. It's true that they can't outright sell your full account information and purchase history—that's illegal under the Gramm-Leach-Bliley Act of 1999. But the law contains a big, fat loophole called "tokenization." Tokenization is the replacement of personally identifying data such as your name or credit card number with an anonymous unique identifier. Basically, as long as credit card companies assign you a token in place of your name, they're allowed to sell your data to whomever they like.

"Here's a list of the IP addresses of nine hundred thousand people who like to buy sweatpants," they might say, handing the tally to a hungry marketer. "That will be three million dollars, please." Although the receiving entity can't see your name, the data they're handed still enables them to track your online movements and feed you advertisements for products they know you buy. The three largest credit card companies in the United

States—American Express, MasterCard, and Visa—have all admitted to this behavior, and frankly, they have little reason to stop.

Under the Gramm-Leach-Bliley Act, companies can sell their customers' financial data, including credit card information, the date and amount of your transactions, and the personal data you give up when you apply for the credit card. Consumers have no privacy unless they take steps to "opt out," which is often a hassle. As a result, our financial information is being bought, sold, traded, and curated at an ever-accelerating pace.[122]

Even more unnerving is that credit bureaus themselves are some of the largest sellers of consumer data. The three major national credit bureaus in the US are Equifax, Experian, and TransUnion. They are private firms that collect payment histories on everyone who gets a loan or a credit card. Banks send them the information for free and then buy it back in the form of a credit report for someone applying for a loan. Your credit history not only determines how much you can borrow, but how much interest you'll have to pay.

The term "credit bureau" might lead you to believe that these organizations are operated and overseen by the government, but in fact, most are private, for-profit businesses. And as it turns out, one of their biggest revenue streams is the sale of consumer data. Each of the three companies make over a billion dollars a year, with Experian leading the way with revenues of $5.2 billion in 2020.[123] TransUnion followed with $2.7 billion in revenue,[124] and Equifax reported $1.1 billion in 2020.[125]

The market for your information gets really hot when you apply for a loan. The credit bureau gets a request for your credit history and then instantly lets other lenders know what you're up to. Bang! Here come the competing offers. Unfortunately, a lot of these operators don't have great reputations. The names of their companies are almost identical to the names of legitimate lenders, while their websites are often a minefield of vague assertions and lousy spelling and grammar.[126]

I've seen this in action. For example, a few years ago, I was contacted by a home-buying hopeful who'd found me via my YouTube channel. One of the first things he said to me was "Jen, I love your videos. They're so clear and grounded. I know you won't screw me over." Gratified that he'd gained so much from my content, I had him fill out an application for a loan, and then I contacted the credit bureau to pull his credit report. A week later, he called me up again—this time to cuss me out. "Jen, ever since I filled out your application, those idiots over at XYZ Mortgage have not stopped calling me. Why are you selling my data?"

I was horrified. I mean, call-your-senator, write-your-congressman horrified. Until then, I hadn't realized that when you fill out a lending application, credit bureaus will often sell your data to third-party lenders as "trigger leads"—that is, leads triggered by the customer actively pursuing a loan. Depending on your loan type and credit score, the bureaus might make thirty dollars, fifty dollars, even seventy dollars off your information—but all you get is a barrage of unsolicited calls: "Hey, I hear you're looking for a mortgage. Let's talk about rates."

This practice is perfectly legal, by the way. Gross, but legal. The theory goes that it's good for the consumer to be offered multiple rates. I don't buy that theory at all because the companies most likely to buy these leads are also the most deceptive. They'd have to be, wouldn't they, to pretend they *just so happened* to obtain your information by sheer magic? Meanwhile, the original mortgage lenders—people like me, who are just trying to find an honest rate for applicants—lose the trust of our clients because they believe we've sold them out. I've brought this issue to the attention of legislators and mortgage experts for years, and the only consistent response I've received is "Sorry, Jen. They can do what they want. We have zero control over this."

Maybe the problem is that *not enough of us* are writing and calling Congress. Political will comes from the people. What do you think your senator or representative should know about data brokering and trigger leads?

The sad fact is that if you have good credit, or if you are getting a VA or FHA loan, you're going to be sold to the highest bidder. (Your quickest way to stop this practice is to simply hang up on any lender who calls you out of the blue. Better yet, say, "Jen Beeston said to let you know buying leads is for trash lenders," and *then* hang up!)

So we've seen that advertisers can easily track your online transactions, either by using their own cookies or by buying your purchase history from third parties—even third parties you might believe you can trust. But what happens if you take your business outside the online sphere?

REAL-WORLD TRACKING

Here's the first thing you should remember about buying in the real world: your credit card company is most likely already selling your data to third parties. So if you use any digital means to purchase goods or services, our battalion of boardroom marketers is going to hear about it. "Fine," you might be thinking, "I'll just pay in cash." However, even if you cancel all your cards and payment services, marketers still have ways to monitor where you shop and what you buy.

For example, a few years ago, I was browsing at the *New York Post* pop-up Christmas shop in Manhattan and found some fantastic towels—so fluffy, like hugging a baby lamb. Man, I wanted those towels. But when I took them to the register, things got weird.

The cashier asked me for my email address. I declined, as I always do. He claimed he couldn't do the transaction without it. I called him on his BS, but he insisted that the system absolutely required an email address, and there was no way for me to buy those towels without it.

Now, a smart salesperson would just input a fake email address and capture the sale. But this guy was holding my fluffy-lamb towels ransom, trying to bully me into handing over my email address so some faceless corporation could track my purchases. Personally, I don't need towels that badly, so I left them behind. But a lot of shoppers, even if they initially resisted, would just go along with it.

I've got another story for you. This past summer, while visiting Boston, I was sweltering and stopped into an iced-tea shop for a cold drink. There was nobody inside except a couple of servers behind the counter. On the wall, there was a large tablet with a sign that said, "Order Here."

I asked one of the servers, "Do I really need to put my order in the tablet? I could just tell you."

"Sorry," they replied. "All our orders have to go through the system."

So, while they stood and watched, I punched my order for a nine dollar iced tea into the tablet. Before I could complete it, the system demanded my phone number so it could "send me alerts about my order."

What alerts? It's only me in the shop. I'm going to watch my order being made.

I tried to enter a fake phone number, and it got rejected. I asked the server, "Do I really have to put my phone number in here? Can't I complete the order without it?"

"Sorry," they said. "That's the way the system is set up."

There was no privacy notice offered. There were no disclosures about how my personal information would be stored or used, and no option to opt-out of third-party data sharing. At a minimum, I knew that if I gave up my number, I'd get texts about iced tea until the end of time: *It's two-for-one day! Bring a friend!* Or *Fifty cents off your next order!* From a shop I visited once, in a city where I don't live. Sure, if I text "STOP," they'll usually stop—but they still have my number on a list they can sell. I didn't need iced tea that badly either.

This type of forced data capture, suggestive selling, and data brokering is everywhere. It's not the cashiers' fault. They're just following store policy. The problem is much further up the food chain, with the decision-makers who set up those data-capture systems, and demand that employees pressure customers for their personal information. Point-of-sale (POS) data-capture systems are heavily marketed to retailers as a valuable tool to understand and enhance their business. The stores are focused on their own bottom line. Protecting your privacy is up to you. Don't give your information up without (at a minimum) a clear privacy policy that includes opt-out provisions.

So how does gathering all this consumer data help corporations target you specifically?

THE DANGERS OF BROKERED DATA

The *New York Times* article about that pregnant teen girl illustrates one point clearly: marketers can and will use your purchase history to draw conclusions about you as a person— and more importantly, as a buyer.

I've had a business page on Facebook for years, and one day I realized that I could target my ads to a shockingly granular degree: not just to my desired zip code, but to people within that zip code by income, job type, educational background, marital status, whether they had children, whether their parents were living or dead, what type of car they drive, and more. Some of those options would clearly violate the Fair Housing Act, so I'd never use them. Facebook has since implemented Fair Housing rules for real estate ads, but it was an interesting rabbit hole to fall down that woke me up to how much data they actually have. I don't know why burglars aren't using it to rob rich people's houses (probably because they can also tell who has a security system). *I am not encouraging a life of crime!* But you should know that you can be targeted based on any aspect of your life.

And that's just me—a layman—clicking a few boxes on a Facebook page. I have a buddy who devises targeted Facebook ads. He and his little company are like assassins when it comes to pinpointing a client's target audience. For example, one of his clients sold implements for washing barber tools. My friend found every person in the United States who either worked as a barber professionally or cut their family's hair at home, identified their individual demographic, and targeted an ad directly at them. He also worked with a company that made swimsuits that changed color when they got wet. Instead of simply ad-blasting all of Facebook as winter ended, he posted ads geographically, timing them to precede each zip code's spring break. Retailers are so eager for this service, and find the results so lucrative, that my friend (only twenty-three years old) makes more than $300,000 *per month.*

A few short years ago, gathering and implementing this kind of data would have been a massive undertaking. But with the power of Facebook's data mining, it takes my friend about ten minutes to target you so precisely that he might as well be dropping *Star Trek* worms into your brain. Now, I used my friend's powers for good. Years ago, he helped me spread my message so that consumers don't get preyed upon. He never promotes dodgy or sketchy products, and never creates ads that are deceptive. He's one of the good guys—but if he can pull that off with his little company, imagine what a major corporation with billions of dollars and hordes of marketers (who aren't all good guys) can do with your personal information.

And, of course, the dangers of sharing your data online don't stop with advertisers.

OTHER PRIVACY RISKS

Maybe you aren't personally susceptible to targeted advertising because you don't shop online. Great, good for you. But there are other ways that freely sharing your data—or simply posting to social media—can disrupt your life.

Everyone's heard of cases where digital data has led to the capture of scammers, cheats, or even murderers. For example, police used phone-location data to help zero in on the suspect in the 2018 serial bombings in Austin, Texas.[127] I'm not going to begrudge the cops their chance to snag a domestic terrorist. But however you feel about the police or the crime, consider this: What if it's not the good guys behind those metaphorical binoculars, watching out for criminals? What if it's the other way around?

Take my friend Terry. A couple years ago, he went on vacation to Cancun, posted a photo of the scenery, and wrote, "It's so beautiful here." Nothing dangerous, right? He didn't list his location or invite a serial killer to come for a visit. But unbeknownst to Terry, one of his Facebook friends had recently relapsed into a drug habit and was consorting with some very unsavory people. Desperate for money—and knowing Terry was basking in the sunshine—he led his new buddies to Terry's house, where they broke in and stole everything worth selling.

Your real-life scenario could look even darker. Maybe you decide to post a photo of your beautiful spouse and child, announcing,

"It's Henry's first day of school!" This is a pretty typical proud-parent moment—but in the background of the photo, Henry's school logo is visible. Guess what? Pedophiles across the country now know where your child attends school. How hard will it be for them to figure out his schedule?

It's worse than that. The metadata your phone automatically embeds in a photograph (called "Exchangeable image format" or "Exif data") includes geotagging. This location data is so precise, anyone with an internet connection and basic Google skills can learn how to find your house—or even pinpoint your child's bedroom—from anywhere in the world.

If that sounds too paranoid to be believable, consider the less extreme but very real effects of sacrificing your kids' privacy online, and how they feel about it. Students in England have asked Facebook to put a "consent button" on pages so children can report when their parents have posted something about them without their permission. In France, authorities have gone on Facebook to warn parents about posting photos of their children that would violate their privacy and future reputations.[128] Their grown children could one day sue them for putting their security and privacy at risk.[129]

Countless children have been embarrassed by their parents' posts. How many have had to endure harassment or intimidation as a result? The wrong social media post about your child can cause them to face bullies in school.

The editors of the kid-safe video site Jellies.com expressed it perfectly:

You should also be concerned about how others may react to the stuff you share about your child on social media. Whether your child cares about old photos and stories about them on social media, others may be able to use that information to make fun of, insult, and even bully your child as they grow older. What's to stop a peer from sharing a photo that your child finds embarrassing with their own networks? What if that share catches on? It doesn't take much for a photo to go from an inside family joke to gossip fodder for an entire high school.[130]

This book is all about defending your wallet—but ultimately, we all have more important things to protect. If you find yourself reluctant to slow down, reduce your internet traffic, and make each digital choice with care, use this as inspiration: your online choices don't just affect you.

As you ponder that notion, let's start looking for ways to keep our data safe from those who might use it against us.

FIGHT BACK—TOGETHER

The good news is that when it comes to protecting your data, your options are getting better.

Apple recently released a series of tools you can use to prevent apps like Facebook and Snapchat from following your movements around the internet. Of course, Apple was motivated by public outcry, congressional investigations, and pushback from consumers, not by an attack of conscience. These enhanced privacy protections gave them a competitive edge against Android phones and their parent company, Google.

The point is that consumers pushed back, and as a result, you now have the opportunity to use your iPhone to regain control of your data. Android users might have a harder time, since data mining is Google's whole business model.

We can all apply social pressure on platforms and content providers to push back against brainhacked hypertargeting. As a content creator myself, I'm always on the lookout for ways to restrict unethical advertisers from targeting my viewers and readers. This is especially important because anyone viewing my content is likely doing so because they want to invest in real estate, making them prime targets for scammers.

Unfortunately, Facebook and Instagram currently offer creators zero ability to block scammy advertisers, but let's give a shout-out to YouTube for providing more flexibility. At the moment of this writing, I am allowing some ad targeting on my channel as a test, but it's very limited and temporary. For example, I can choose what industries can advertise on my channel. I do not allow any real estate themed advertisements on my channel, along with several other categories that carry higher risk.

Can taking this road have consequences? Of course. For one thing, I'm giving up ad revenue. That's fine with me. Ad revenue has never been a profit center for my business. Monetizing the channel gives me more control over the ads. If it weren't monetized, YouTube could show any ads they wanted, and I'd have no say. I have seen far too many scam ads, and I care about my viewers too much to risk them falling prey to an ad they saw on my channel.

Additionally, as part of educating my viewers, I often post warnings about known scams, as well as invite viewers to call me directly if they see an ad they suspect might be deceptive or lead to a data-capture site. Fraud is only too common in the mortgage-lending field, and if I can donate a five-minute phone call here and there to protect someone, I'll happily do so.

We can all work together and hold one another accountable. We all want the internet to become a safer place to interact, so it's up to us to make it happen. And as we do so, we must also watch each other's backs for our next threat: hucksters, influencers, and fake gurus.

CHAPTER SEVEN

SCAMMERS AND FINANCIAL DEVIANTS

It's not just the algorithms and ads that are hacking your wallet. Everyone wants a piece of your hard-earned cash, so let's talk about some of the ones you are most likely to see on a day-to-day basis.

Picture this: You're lying in bed watching YouTube, when an ad comes up featuring a guy lounging against a Lamborghini in front of a mansion. Bikini-clad women stroke his carefully disheveled hair or toy with his designer lapels.

"I'm twenty-six years old," he tells the camera, "but I made five million dollars this year alone. Want to know how? It's all in my step-by-step course. For an investment of just fifteen hundred dollars"—he squeezes both women closer and throws the camera a wink—"you can change your life overnight."

You'd never tap this ad, right? Although now that you think about it, money is tight lately, and "this guy, twenty-six? Ridiculous!" Nevertheless, your finger hovers over the screen. Is there any chance this guy's legitimate?

Of course not. Guys like this want you to believe they made their millions off of drop-shipping—or any number of other get-rich-quick schemes—when in reality, they're making their money right now, by selling their often worthless how-tos with deceptive marketing.

We already know the internet can be a minefield for the unwary, with advertisers manipulating your emotions, cookies tracking your data, and pay-per-click ads tailored to your life. Let's add another danger to that list: the hucksters, influencers, and fake gurus of the internet world. They're everywhere, and they're selling lifestyles that might tempt anyone.

In this chapter, we're going to talk about how to see through these petty scammers and the masks they wear. And we're going to start by identifying some of the most common, persistent scams out there.

GET-RICH GURUS

The girl-draped playboy we met above is a perfect example of what I'll call a Get-Rich Guru—a scammer selling a course teaching his secrets for gaining wealth. (I say "his" because in my experience, the ones running these scams are almost always male, as are those they target. But don't worry, ladies. We'll get to our own weak points soon enough.) The course might be a how-to guide, set of classes, or series of lectures, but rest assured—there are no true secrets within. What the Get-Rich Guru really wants to sell you is the dream of being wealthy. This is why his sales pitch is almost always accompanied by the same ingredients—an impressive mansion in the background, beautiful women, and a fancy sports car.

What kinds of "secrets" might the Get-Rich Guru be peddling? Most often, some kind of online business that boasts low startup costs, automated operations, and no previous experience required. For example, since the e-commerce boom of the 2000s, drop-shipping has become a popular scheme. Drop-shipping is a perfectly legitimate business model in itself—it's just a way for retailers to have stock shipped directly from the manufacturer to customers instead of keeping inventory themselves. However, the idea is packaged and sold as a sure-fire "proven method" for individuals with no sales experience or business skills to create a lucrative small business with little or no effort.

To be fair, at the beginning of this fad, a few sellers really were making good money by connecting online shoppers with distant manufacturers. But as new sellers entered the field, the original guys watched their profits get eaten away. To regain cash flow, they started devising courses on becoming a drop-shipper—but of course, this flooded the market with even more new sellers. At this point, few new sellers are actually buying products from the source. They are tapping into a network of middlemen and aggregators, each of whom take a slice of the profits. The market opportunity is so diluted that the real money isn't in drop-shipping at all—it's in selling courses.

When someone wants to sell you instructions for getting rich, get into the habit of raising some basic, realistic questions. The moment some tousle-haired Lamborghini boy pops up on your screen, ask yourself this: If this guy's approach to wealth-building is really so lucrative, why on earth is he selling his secrets? Why dilute the market when he could keep all that income himself? There is a reason Warren Buffett is not selling courses.

I've seen similar ads for house-flipping courses: "I made four million dollars this year flipping houses, and you can too! All you need are my ten easy steps to maximum return on your investment." This particular Get-Rich Guru might look a bit more approachable than the first, perhaps mimicking the bearded, flannelled Drew Scotts of the HGTV world. And his approach to building wealth seems so wholesome—you're updating homes for families to buy, for heaven's sake!

But let's break down the Drew Scott lookalike's pitch. In fact, let's do a quick Google search of the real Drew Scott himself. Sure, the Property Brothers have made millions over the years—but that's because they're TV stars. The Get-Rich Guru isn't getting you a TV gig, only offering to teach you how to paint, tile, and spackle. Meanwhile, when it comes to the actual properties you see on home-renovation TV shows, the producers and stars have been slapped with myriad lawsuits over the years complaining about quality.[131] So again, ask yourself: If flipping houses is so easy, why are the professionals constantly being dragged to court over shoddy workmanship? What could these "ten easy steps" possibly be? **When faced with a get-rich-quick course, ask yourself: if this business is so lucrative, why are they selling courses instead?**

Now let's prod the claim that the Get-Rich Guru is even what he pretends to be—that is, rich. It's only too easy to fake wealth or success for the camera. Take Lamborghini Boy. That mansion he's posing in front of? Rented off Airbnb for $450 per night. The girls? Aspiring Instagram models who'll work for "exposure" and free headshots. And the Lamborghini itself? Heck, why stop with a car? For a couple hundred bucks, you can pose for photos with a jet.

Meanwhile, as a mortgage lender, I know how simple it would be for our Drew Scott wannabe to fake a flip. He never even has to leave his house.

Here's how the scam works:

- Download some online photos of home listings and remodels from several websites and different areas of the country.
- Put together a series of social posts that say things like, "We just bought this fixer-upper for $150,000! Let's see if we can double our money."
- Claim you are a master flipper.
- Buy a couple hundred thousand fake followers and likes.
- Create an engagement group page.
- Once the page is full of content of "your success," your fake followers, likes, and comments, then start advertising your courses.

There are no addresses listed for the properties. There is no way to verify you bought them at all. The average person will look at your page and think you are an expert. Course sold! Just like that, a Get-Rich Guru is born.

The same type of fakery can easily be done with any product or service. Ready for a real-life story? When my son was in eighth grade, he and his friend created an Instagram profile for an imaginary railway company they named "R&R Railroad." They posted content about new trains being built, their company culture, planned service routes and amenities, employee of the month, and anything else a real corporation might post. They grabbed pictures from the web and repurposed them. They copied the wording and tone from real corporate accounts so the captions would sound authentic.

People started leaving comments, asking when R&R was coming to their town, and how they could be the first to know! These were middle school students playing a prank, and adults fell for it. Faking is far too easy in today's tech-enhanced world.

SPOT THE RED FLAGS

Think you might be looking at a Get-Rich Guru? Take these steps:

1. If their pitch features an expensive sports car, move on. Wealthy people don't generally advertise their wealth to sell you things—it attracts too much dangerous attention. If the guy running the ad feels the need to lean against a

Lamborghini, that Lamborghini ain't his (or if it is, he got it with your course tuition instead of through the methods he's teaching you).

2. **If they're selling "secrets," don't listen.** If the drop-shipping fad taught us anything, it's this: any "trade secret" worth selling is already too worthless to buy. The knowledge they're sharing is already several years past its best-by date, and that's why they need money from you.

3. **Do twenty minutes of Googling.** What kind of actual work is involved in this money-making scheme? Unless you've inherited wealth or won the lottery, getting rich is not fast and easy—and anyone who says differently just wants your money. Intrigued by the notion of flipping houses, for example? Great. There is money to be made if you do it properly and can bankroll the risk. Get on your laptop and find the truth: that house-flipping is *hard work* with high up-front costs and no guaranteed return on your investment. Lawsuits are common. Failure is common. There are no sure bets.

My point? Strip out your emotions, examine each pitch logically, and take the time to research any venture before buying into some get-rich-quick scheme. This advice applies whether you're dealing with a Get-Rich Guru or his even sleazier brother, the Gaslight Guru.

DOWN THE GARDEN PATH

A Gaslight Guru isn't primarily after your money. Sometimes they will take your money, sure. Other times they offer their advice and "expertise" for free. Their real objective is to manipulate you into making choices—such as disclosing personal data or buying products or stocks—that will benefit them financially.

These predatory online creators present themselves as experts in their fields, but they don't have the credentials or work experience to back up their claims. For example, a YouTube video recently popped up on my feed entitled something like "How to Get a Better Quote from a Mortgage Lender." I was instantly intrigued. Obviously, the creator was competing for the same viewership as I am, and judging by his sheer number of followers, he was beating me out. So I decided to dig a bit deeper. Many lenders have software we can use to review how many loans others are closing, so I pulled up this guy's numbers.

His grand total was four. Not four loans closed this week, month, or even year—four loans *ever*. My apologies to all his subscribers, but this definitely wasn't the person to turn to for mortgage advice.

A few weeks later, I came across a similar pitch from another mortgage-lending "professional." "Yo, yo, yo, listen up," he started his pitch. "Any lender that says you can't get financing, they're just not as smart as me. Why do you think I have cars like this?" He gestured to the—surprise, surprise—Lamborghini sitting behind him. "If I wasn't amazing at my job, it wouldn't exist."

This guy had thousands of followers, but as I've mentioned, I fundamentally distrust anyone leaning on a Lamborghini. I was getting serious scumball vibes. So I decided to follow his links and check out his lending history as well.

What do you know? It turns out, this joker doesn't even do mortgage loans at all. Both of these guys are in the lead-generation business, not the mortgage business. If you click their links, you get sent to a data-collection form, just like those sketchy search results we looked at back in Chapter One. Your information is then farmed out to actual lenders, and they get paid a fee for funneling interested borrowers to their client companies. Neither of them needs to know the first thing about mortgage loans. They're the human equivalent of pop-up ads—but without the legal disclaimers "this is a paid promotion" or "results not typical." They're just commercials pretending to be content.

Of course, a Gaslight Guru can specialize in just about anything, not just mortgage loans. Ever seen those guys hyping specific stocks online—or worse yet, cryptocurrencies? "Hey y'all, you've gotta buy in right now. Get in while you can, because this rocket is going to the moon!" When you hear claims like these, then just as you would with a Get-Rich Guru, you need to take a moment and ask yourself, "Why is this person sharing this secret insider information? How does it benefit him?" In this case, the Gaslight Guru is most likely planning a "pump and dump"—that is, he wants people like us to purchase this stock and pump up its price. Then he'll get all the richer when he dumps his own shares.

The current fad for trading nonfungible tokens (NFTs) as an alternative way of collecting art means that many companies will pay creators to promote the NFTs they're offering. I have had over sixty-five NFT companies contact me this year alone to pitch their product on my YouTube channel. It's big business.

FUN FACT

NFTs are a way of using blockchain technology to permanently "mark" a single copy of a digital file (like an image or song) and prove ownership of that unique copy. Of course, an infinite number of other copies could exist. It is a conceptual value, and people are willing to pay for it—up to a point. Some investment advisors consider NFTs the ultimate example of the "greater fool principle" at work: you can always make money on an overvalued investment, as long as you can find a greater fool than you to take it off your hands.

In March 2021, Jack Dorsey created an NFT of the first tweet ever published on Twitter. It sold to a cryptocurrency CEO for $2.9 million. Remember, anyone can still see that tweet online, or make a copy of it at any time, for free. In April 2022, the Dorsey NFT went back on the market listed at $48 million, but the initial round of bids barely got up to $280.[133] Two hundred and eighty bucks, period. In a second round, bids rose to the thousands, but the owner decided not to sell at such a loss. Since the bids were made in a cryptocurrency with a constantly shifting value, it's hard to nail down a specific price. Various sources quote the highest bid as between $6,000 and $10,000.[134] #buyerbeware.

In 2021, a digital collage called *Everydays: The First 5000 Days* by the artist Beeple was auctioned by Christie's for $69.3 million, making it the most expensive NFT ever sold to a single owner (so far).[135] A print copy of the same images can be bought as a hardback book for about seventy dollars.

Every one of the NFT proposals I received offered *at least* a thousand dollars per post. Clearly, I would never do that. But how many people can turn away an easy $1,000 for a one-minute video post? Every one of those sponsored posts is helping a shady speculator pump and dump their pixel collections.

SPOT THE RED FLAGS

Whether the charismatic "expert" online is offering you advice on finances, marriage, mental health, religion, or anything else, it only makes sense for you to do two things: ask yourself how they benefit from this arrangement, and look them up to see if their credentials are legitimate.

1. **Follow the money.** Let's be clear—there are wonderful, legitimate resources out there on a whole host of topics, and monetizing valuable content is a fair exchange. But in order to determine whether the content is actually valuable, it helps to figure out how this content creator actually makes their money. By working at their business—or by working people like you?

2. **Look for outside verification of their skills.** The quickest way to reveal a Gaslight Guru is to see what their actual qualifications are. When you Google this person, can you find proof from unrelated sources that they're qualified in their area of supposed expertise—industry memberships and awards, recognition in well-known publications, degrees from real schools, or jobs at real companies? Real experts are easy to find in a Google search. If all you find are self-generated articles and videos, odds are that their supposed credentials are trash.

3. **Double-check their assertions.** In a similar vein, don't take a Gaslight Guru's claims of peer validation as gospel. They might brag, "I'm a financial expert—I've appeared in *Forbes*." But how exactly did they appear? Did they author an article? Get spotlighted as an authority in their field? Or simply take out an ad so they could make this very claim? We see a lot of this with *Forbes* for other countries. I even had someone try to sell me on why I should be in *Forbes Monaco*. Yup, Monaco—where I don't live or work, and never have.

A Gaslight Guru's scam can unravel quickly if you shine a spotlight too closely on their claims. The same holds true for his warmer, fuzzier cousin, the Home-Business Idealist.

WORK-FROM-HOME KITS

Ladies, I told you our time would come. This scammer's pitch tends to be less "Let's get you some fast cars and half-naked women!" and more "Let's get you *#Blessed* with *#Abundance* while working from home with your kids, *#Girlboss!*" Unsurprisingly, the target audience of the Home-Business Idealist tends to be stay-at-home moms.

I've personally seen the Home-Business Idealist in action. When I was straight out of college, I got a telemarketing job for a company that sold medical-billing kits. The idea was that people could buy a kit, work from home as a medical biller, and make $10,000 a month. Every day, I was supposed to answer the phone and have this cringey, scripted conversation:

Me: "Thanks a million for calling! Isn't this a great day to start your life and secure your future with your family?"

Caller: "Um. Yes, I guess so. I saw your ad. What do I need to do to get set up?"

Me: "We're going to provide you everything you need to set up your medical-billing business. That will be a thousand dollars."

Caller: "A thousand? That seems like a lot."

Me: "This is nothing compared to the money you will be making.

Imagine how you are going to change your family's life! What credit card would you like to put that on? If it helps, I can break it into four installments. I really don't want you to miss out on changing your family's lives."

I say this was the conversation I was *supposed* to have because in reality, I could never make myself say the words. It was unethical. If potential buyers showed any hesitation, the successful sales-people at this organization would make this software sound like it came straight from God: "Oh Nancy, don't you worry about a thing. All you have to do is give me that credit card—couldn't be easier. Let's go ahead and change your life, girl."

My talks went more like this: "Okay, if you really want this stuff, it's going to be a thousand bucks. But you know it's just the software, right? You'll still have to find the doctors to bill on your own. You are going to have to build the business, and that can be hard."

I only lasted three days before I quit. I would rather live on ramen noodles and goldfish crackers than rip people off.

SPOT THE RED FLAGS

The Home-Business Idealist wants to sell you the idea that a good job and financial freedom are worth whatever price they're asking. So once again, take a moment to consider their offer with a critical eye:

1. **Are they really selling everything you'd need?** What made the medical-billing kits compelling to buyers was the idea of taking control of their time and money, all while staying at home with their families. But what buyers didn't under-

stand—what my bosses went out of their way to hide—was that owning the software and actually using it to make money were two very different things. A legitimate small business has all sorts of economic and legal considerations, from local business licenses, to liability insurance, to reporting self-employment income, to actually getting clients. Those medical-billing kits didn't cover any of those issues. Most WFH kits don't.

2. **Can someone in this field actually make this much money?** Take the time to do some math. How much billing would you actually have to do in a month to recover the promised ten grand? Is it even mathematically possible? If the numbers don't add up, then neither does this scheme.

3. **If you were buying the ingredients of this kit separately, would it still cost this much?** What exactly is in this kit, and could you purchase something comparable elsewhere for cheaper?

Keep your eyes wide open to protect your cash from the Home-Business Idealist—and her even bigger, shinier offspring, the Multilevel Marketing Maven. After all, it's common sense to be wary of strangers. But what if the person asking for your money is a friend or family member?

DOUBLE-DIAMOND PLATINUM-LEVEL SCAMS

Men might be tempted by bikinis and Lamborghinis, but nothing grabs money from a woman's pocket faster than another woman—we'll call her the Overzealous Sales Friend. If you've somehow missed the explosion of multilevel marketing companies—a.k.a., MLMs—over the last few decades, let me give you a quick explanation.

According to the Federal Trade Commission, multilevel marketing, also called "network marketing" or "direct marketing," involves selling products to your family, friends, and others. You can sell from your home, your car, your computer, or even by going door-to-door.

Some MLMs will only pay you for the sales you make, but others won't pay until you recruit others to join your sales network. Either way, most people who join MLMs make little or no money, according to the FTC. The company you're selling for often requires that you purchase a certain amount of product at set intervals, even if you already have sufficient inventory. Few sellers ever qualify for the lavish prizes offered for certain sales goals. The scam requires everyone to keep recruiting new people and giving the main distributor a steady supply of new recruits—and their money—rolling into the business.[136]

How is this legal? Ten years ago, MLMs successfully lobbied for exclusion from FTC "business opportunity" rules that require businesses to support their income claims and disclose to potential investors whether they've been sued—for fraud, say. This freed MLMs to say whatever they wanted to get people to sign up.[137]

Firms like LuLaRoe, the makers of brightly colored clothing, took full advantage of this freedom, recruiting individual agents to sell their goods and recruit others to do the same. It launched in 2012, and by 2016 it was one of the largest firms in the multilevel marketing industry with over $1 billion in sales.[138] By 2017, it had over eighty thousand independent distributors.[139]

LuLaRoe was declared a pyramid scheme by the Washington

State Attorney General in 2019 but had already faced heavy criticism and lawsuits over its business model and the quality of its merchandise, which were said to hold up about as well as "wet toilet paper."[140] In addition to lawsuits from distributors and the state of Washington, LuLaRoe was also sued by its manufacturer, who claimed the company hadn't paid its bills for seven months and accused founders Mark and DeAnne Stidham of hiding profits in shell companies.

LuLaRoe required its distributors to make an initial investment of $5,000 to $9,000 for goods and marketing materials and encouraged sellers to keep around $20,000 worth of products on hand. Since most of its distributors were from poor rural areas and didn't have much, the company actually advised some female distributors to sell their breast milk to raise money to buy more inventory. Talk about multitasking.

Distributors earned revenue from direct sales and commissions on the number of "downline" sellers they recruited. Sellers were trained to use different sales approaches, including pop-up boutiques, live-streamed sales events on Facebook, and hosting parties for potential buyers. According to LuLaRoe's 2015 income disclosure statement, the average annual commission distributors earned from downline distributors was eighty-five dollars. Let me repeat that: eighty-five freaking dollars *per year*.

LuLaRoe's sudden rise and subsequent legal problems inspired a documentary miniseries on Amazon Prime titled *LuLaRich*. You absolutely should watch this. It is fascinating and heartbreaking, and will stop you from ever falling into an MLM.

Beachbody, another multilevel marketing company, started in

1998 selling exercise DVDs. By 2007, it had transformed into what *Forbes* magazine called "a social media-fueled pyramid seller of health shakes." In 2018, the company had more than 340,000 independent "coaches" selling the company's videos, shakes, and supplements online to people who want to lose weight.

Beachbody sells fitness and nutrition programs—including daily instruction and eating plans—to get you in shape. It offers a variety of online workouts, from yoga to kickboxing, that you can perform in your home. "The playbook goes something like this: Lose weight with Beachbody by doing the at-home workouts and drinking the shakes," wrote Lauren Debter in *Forbes*. "Share it on social media. Use your story to sell products and recruit new customers and coaches. Repeat."

By many accounts, the exercises are effective.[141] However, Beachbody started looking like a pyramid scheme when it started peddling its sugary Shakeology and other nutritional supplements. What made Shakeology so appealing? The company pushed it as a kind of magical elixir that not only allowed you to lose weight but also prevented mental decline, slowed the aging process, removed toxins, and prevented heart disease and cancer.[142] The company called it a "daily dose of dense nutrition." It cost $130 for a month's supply.

While some Beachbody coaches have done exceptionally well, the average Beachbody coach in 2016 made just $3,233 a year. By 2020, the average coach made about thirty-seven dollars per month—that's just $444 a year. To keep your standing with the company, you need to sell or buy about fifty-five dollars' worth of products a month, so distributors are incentivized to buy inventory they can't sell in order to stay in good standing.

Beachbody has faced its share of legal challenges. In addition to paying $3.6 million to settle a lawsuit alleging that the company charged customer credit cards for automatic renewals without written consent, customers have complained that it's difficult to cancel subscriptions or get a refund for products sold after their expiration date has passed.

When Beachbody switched from selling DVD workouts to a streaming model, sales dropped 25 percent and triggered a mass exodus of distributors. This forced the company to focus more on selling their shake subscriptions, which prompted authorities to crack down on the wild claims Beachbody made about its drink mix. Now California bars the company from making any claim that isn't backed by scientific evidence.[143]

So, when an Overzealous Sales Friend targets you, she's usually looking to get your money in one of two ways: selling to you or recruiting you. Often it is both.

SELLING TO YOU

In my experience, the Overzealous Sales Friend will usually reach out via social media, starting her pitch with something like this: "Hey Steph, remember when we were in algebra together? It's been so long! Anyway, I'm planning to try and lose some weight through Beachbody, and I wondered if you might want to join up. It's super fun, and the shakes are just delicious."

Her implied insult to your weight aside, maybe you do remember those good times in algebra. Maybe you've been following Overzealous Sales Friend on social media and know she's going through a challenging time, or you always just wanted to hang with her. Either way, you might be tempted to support her and buy a few shakes. After all, this isn't some Get-Rich Guru. She's your old friend. What could it hurt?

Your Overzealous Sales Friend might not have evil intentions, but she's still trying to separate you from your hard-earned money. Anyone who is trying to separate you from your money is a salesperson. So drop her in that category now.

Okay, are you still somewhat interested? Before you open your wallet, take a breath.

BEFORE YOU BUY

Ask yourself the following questions:

1. **Has your Overzealous Sales Friend been using this product for a long time?** If your friend has been a fan of this line of clothing or skincare products for years, it's likely she's a true believer in the product. Her testimonial might be worth listening to, even if you don't ultimately decide to buy. If, however, she's just jumped on this bandwagon recently, it's likely she's only here for the money. Take her word with a grain of salt.

2. **Is this a brand I would buy in a store?** Answer this question truthfully. Would you seek out this product—not this type of product, but this specific product—if your friend weren't shoving it under your nose? Think about it. If you don't crave those shakes, yearn for those scented candles, or wish those LuLaRoes were stocked at your local clothing store—this product isn't worth your time or money.

3. **Is this item priced correctly?** Consider the quality of this

product with a critical eye. If you saw it on a store shelf, would you realistically pay the asking price?

4. **Are you ready for your Overzealous Sales Friend to hit you up every week with offers to buy more?** Because let's be clear—this is what you're signing up for. Salespeople know it costs a lot less to keep an existing customer than seduce a new one. So if you're not fully in love with the quality and price of this product, nip this thing in the bud right now.

Of course, it's possible your Overzealous Sales Friend doesn't just want to sell you on shakes or makeup or leggings. She might want to sell you on *selling*.

RECRUITING YOU

Here's another variation of that first sales pitch: "Hey Steph, I haven't talked to you in years! Oh my God, I'm having so much success selling through Beachbody. You should totally come join me. You're so beautiful and charming—you'd make a ton of money, I just know it!"

Again, you might have a dozen reasons to be tempted by your Overzealous Sales Friend's invitation. Maybe you've seen her posts bragging that sales are going so well, her husband has now quit his job. Maybe you've seen all those perfectly posed photos of her family with their new Lamborghini (or jet). Maybe you just hate to leave a friend hanging. But before you jump in head-first, consider this little reality check.

BEFORE YOU BUY IN

First and foremost, I consider myself an educator, but technically, I am a salesperson. So when I say the following statements, please understand that they come from a voice of experience:

1. **Successful salespeople don't have to sell hard to their family and friends.** I would never reach out to my old college buddies to say, "Hey Becky, are you interested in a mortgage loan?" I don't have to—because people are actually interested in what I'm selling. If a friend is reaching out to get you to buy her shakes, candles, dresses, or whatever, it's because she doesn't have someone else to sell to. And if *she* doesn't have someone to sell to, you don't have anyone to sell to either.

2. **If there's no barrier to entry, there's no reason to enter.** Here's another message I've never sent to an old friend: "Hey Becky, I'm making tons of money as a mortgage lender. Want to jump onboard? It's so easy!" People do not get rich doing "easy" things—after all, if anyone can do a job, then *everyone* would be doing that job. If your friend is offering you an easy way to make money, get suspicious.

3. **Sales is hard—and the product matters.** Do a quick Google search. MLMs are encouraged (but not required) to publish income disclosure statements—but if they do, those figures are required to reflect the typical earnings of the average distributor. From that, you can figure for yourself the percentage of salespeople in this MLM that actually turn a profit. Unless you're a statistical rarity, buying a huge "sales kit" of subpar protein shakes is going to lose you money.

A 2017 study by the Consumer Awareness Institute (CAI) concluded that 99 percent of the people involved as sellers in the multilevel marketing industry lose money. A separate survey of more than a thousand MLM sellers found that most made less than seventy cents an hour. One in five sellers never made a sale, and six out of ten sellers earned less than $500 after five years of work.[144]

Jon Taylor, the researcher who conducted the CAI study, analyzed 350 MLMs and found that each one of them paid commissions to "a tiny percentage" of the MLMs' "top-of-the-pyramid promoters." In other words, the early promoters made a lot of money by recruiting more and more sellers, but 99 percent of those sellers never earned much of anything.

"Our studies, along with those done by other independent analysts (not connected to the MLM industry), clearly prove that MLM as a business model—with its endless chain of recruitment of participants as primary customers—is flawed, unfair, and deceptive," Taylor wrote. "Worldwide feedback suggests it is also extremely viral, predatory and harmful to many participants."[145]

Let me be clear: if you buy into an MLM, odds are you will end up in a worse financial place than you are now. So now that you've faced this inevitable fact, how are you going to stave off all those Overzealous Sales Friends out there?

SHIELDS UP

We've all received those "Hey Jennifer, long time!" messages and known a sales pitch was coming. The responses below might not be pretty, but in my experience, they're effective at keeping MLM salespeople at bay. And after all, protecting your money is the whole point of this book. So when your Overzealous Sales Friend comes sniffing around, try having one of these maneuvers at the ready:

1. **Set a firm personal policy.** Let's start with the most straight-forward route: "Sorry Lana, but I never involve myself in MLMs. I just don't trust them. All the best with this, though." Most salespeople don't keep pushing if you shut them down quickly and firmly.

2. **Become spontaneously allergic.** Yep, I'm recommending that you straight-up lie: "Sorry, Lana, but protein powder makes me break out in hives. My system is so oversensitive to everything!"

3. **Hit mute.** If our hypothetical Lana won't stop overposting on social media, quietly hit that mute button for a while. Since she's no way of knowing you've turned off her mic, her feelings will be spared, and you won't have to keep cringing at her pitches.

4. **Deflect.** Anytime Lana reaches out to you directly, try ignoring her message. If she presses you on your lack of response, say, "You sent me something? Well, you know me—I barely know how to use Facebook Messenger."

If these methods sound a bit heartless to you, or if you find yourself sympathizing with your Overzealous Sales Friend and her desperate bids for your business, remember this: just because someone else is trying really hard or struggling financially, that doesn't mean you need to endanger your own finances by buying junk you don't need.

And speaking of junk you don't need, let's talk about our final scammer of the chapter, one of the most prolific peddlers of garbage on the internet.

ASPIRATIONAL INSPO

I don't need to invent a nickname for this scammer. We already know her by her preferred moniker: the Influencer.

You might have heard of Johanna Olsson, the travel influencer who Photoshopped herself into a series of photos of Paris. The photos were nice but unrealistic. In one, she appears to be levitating. In another, she has a precise halo around her head, suggesting a digital cutout. Eventually, she admitted to altering the photos but was angered by the attention her fakery attracted among her five hundred thousand Instagram followers and thirty-three thousand YouTube subscribers. "I just wanted to make (it) clear that I was in Paris, but I did photoshop the background," she said, "but I'm not going to take them down because...they're nice pictures." She also said her sleight of hand was commonplace among influencers.[146]

So true. One influencer from Buenos Aires was accused of faking her travel pics when her followers noticed the same cloud formations regardless of where she was traveling. The influencer, Tupi Saravia, was so popular (she has three hundred thousand followers) that "even the clouds follow her around," according to one observer.[147]

Filters and video editing have become so effective, you could make a garden shed look like Buckingham Palace. It's become incredibly easy for people to lead false lives online, cultivating misleading personas that have us salivating over their fitness, beauty, wealth, or adventurousness. But how much of what we see is real? Let's take a minute to look at why the Influencer is incentivized to lie, how financial sponsorships play into her choices, and how we can see through the fraying seams of her online mask.

SPONSORSHIP: THE HIDDEN INFLUENCE

Word-of-mouth advertising—such as when a friend recommends a restaurant—has far more power than traditional advertising. You trust it more because the person promoting the restaurant has nothing to gain by telling you about those fantastic cheese raviolis.

That trust is what has allowed the emergence of "influencers" as a major marketing channel in this age of social media. At a time when people search out online reviews for cotton swabs before making a purchase at Rite-Aid, influencers can hold a lot of sway. In an annual survey conducted across the globe by the Edelman Trust Barometer, more than half of the respondents declared that "individuals are more believable than institutions and a company's social media page is more believable than advertising."[148]

Influencers make their living via sponsorship, which means that every time they gush about some new product, it's because someone's putting money in their pocket. Is selling products for a living unethical? Of course not. There are influencers who actually use and like the products they promote. They tend to have long-term relationships with those brands, and an organic connection between the brand and the topic they cover. You might see a food vlogger endorse cookware, or a tech geek partner with a VPN service. Those endorsements aren't manipulative in the way I'm talking about.

But consider this: Sponsors want to spend their money well. If they're going to send $500 worth of diet pills or exercise equipment to some Influencer, they're not going to choose someone overweight so they can prove how well the products work.

They're going to choose someone who's already fit—someone who can make you believe the products are effective *without using them once.*

Meanwhile, your typical Influencer has little to no reason to turn this money down. Most aren't carefully cultivating a long-term brand; they're taking whatever cash comes their way to survive the lean years and grow their careers. Even Influencers who start out with pure intentions can be brought low once sponsors get involved. For example, say you love a particular Influencer—let's call her Claire—because her yoga workouts make you feel refreshed and uplifted. She might have started making videos because she honestly believes in the power of yoga to improve people's lives. But if one month, her videos suddenly change—if she starts promoting fitness equipment one week, then a diet pill the next, then sports bras and a special green powder after that—know that Claire has been bought. She is no longer thinking about the good of her followers but about building her business. Pushing products is now her job, as surely as it's the job of an actress on a commercial.

Let's get real—the word "influencer" is just another word for "salesperson." Most of society views salespeople as a scourge, like those sleazy car sellers that keep rusted-out bumpers attached with duct tape. Why are Influencers any different?

The products that influencers openly endorse are just the tip of the iceberg. Many influencers are less than honest about which sponsors are actually paying them for their supposedly off-the-cuff, word-of-mouth recommendations. Some merely retweet endorsement texts written by their sponsor, and many others are flaunting federal rules by hiding the fact that they're getting paid for their tweets and posts.[149] FTC rules require that if you have a "material relationship" to a product you're posting about, you must disclose it in the captions by using words like "ad" or "sponsored." But by one estimate, 93 percent of the celebrity endorsements you see on social media violate Federal Trade Commission fair-practice rules.[150]

In 2017, the FTC sent out notices to scores of celebrities, influencers, and marketers reminding them that they need to "conspicuously disclose" their relationships to brands when promoting products over social media.[151] No one paid much attention. Then, in 2020, the FTC fined the detox tea company Teami $1 million and publicly chastised Cardi B for not disclosing her paid endorsements.

Still, influencing is huge and growing. The industry grew from $1.7 billion in 2016 to $16.4 billion in 2022.[152] An estimated 93 percent of marketers have used influencers, and consumers seem to favor influencer-generated pitches over branded content. As a result, even micro-influencers—pitchmen with a relatively small pack of followers—can make $20,000 to $40,000 a year. Their followers seem to be okay with the fact that their influencer is getting paid, but they do expect them to be up front about who their sponsors are.[153] But even when they are, consumers have a hard time distinguishing a sponsored post from a personal recommendation, particularly when the influencer buries their disclosures.

Today, any influencer worth their weight in hashtags is making money from the effort. Those who aren't getting paid are often *pretending* like they have sponsors in an effort to show what they can do and land a gig with a bonafide brand.[154] Their motto: "Fake it till you make it."

According to the *Atlantic* magazine, "Lifestyle blogging is all about seamlessly monetizing your good taste and consumer choices, which means it can be nearly impossible for laypeople to tell if an influencer genuinely loves a product, is being paid to talk about it, or just wants to be paid to talk about it."

It's hard to tell how many influencers actually turn down sponsorships in an effort to keep their objectivity and credibility with their followers. A survey conducted by Activate, a "fully end-to-end influencer marketing platform," found that the main reason influencers turn down sponsorship offers is because they couldn't agree on payment or were already endorsing a competing brand. "Desire to maintain credibility" was not even an option Activate asked about.[155]

WHEN SPONSORS COME CALLING

At this point you might be thinking, "Jennifer, we aren't stupid. We know these online personas aren't realistic. Are you really going to pretend your own social media presence is 100 percent accurate?"

Of course I'm not! The Jennifer Beeston I promote on YouTube and TikTok is way more poised and put-together than I am, since I never make a video without doing my hair and thinking through my message first. But here's the difference between me and a sponsor-fueled Influencer: The primary purpose of my online presence is to educate. I do not make my money by promoting products on the internet. In fact, I only ever mention a specific product or business in one of my videos if I truly believe it will benefit viewers—never because that brand is paying me.

Yes, my content raises my public profile, and I get business as a result. But I'd get a lot *more* traffic if I resorted to the cheap lead-generation and faux-inspo tactics I'm calling out here. You see, I understand how their tricks work, which means I could perform those tricks as well or better. But I don't, because I'd rather make an honest living and sleep at night.

To balance out my polished persona on my professional channels, I keep it real on my Instagram Stories. I have a life outside of mortgages, and it certainly isn't always polished. I like to eat flaming cheese. I aspire to cook but I could burn water. (No, really—I did a cooking tutorial for baked potatoes.) My dog has zero chill. The way my hair looks when I'm surfing is *not* the way it looks at the office. I think it's important to put some authenticity out there.

Not that I haven't considered sponsorship when brands were actually relevant to my field. I was once contacted by a company that wanted me to endorse their debt-consolidation services. "Interesting," I said. "Send me a demo so I can see how this works." I didn't want to feed my viewers some fake financial product designed to steal their identities. Alarm bells started ringing in my head when the would-be sponsor completely ignored my request for a demo. Instead, they jumped straight to my compensation: "We'd like you to promote us in fifteen social media posts and ten videos. How much would you like us to pay you for that?"

Fortunately, it wasn't hard to resist the offer because, as I mentioned, influencing isn't my job—selling mortgages is. If I turn down a sponsor, that puts me in zero financial danger. But someone who makes their living as an Influencer? Getting an offer like this—or from a bra manufacturer or video game company, which I've also had—would feel like they've finally made it. A few thousand dollars a month could change their life. Most people are not going to stop to think about how this "partnership" could harm their audience, or their long-term brand growth.

SPOT THE RED FLAGS

In practice, seeing through an Influencer is similar to seeing through a Gaslight Guru: question their motives, and verify their claims:

1. Take the "guilty until proven innocent" approach. Remember that the fake-follower industry is thriving. Instead of thinking, "This person has two million followers, they must be legit," assume those followers are fake. In fact, you should assume every Influencer is actively lying to you—about their appearance, lifestyle, habits, beliefs, and more—until you verify their authenticity through reviews on multiple sites.
2. Watch for mathematical red flags. Let's say you follow Jim and Penny, a husband-and-wife duo who claim to make their entire living from crafting—but live in a fabulous $10 million dollar mansion. Crafting did not earn that mansion. Advertising did. Ask yourself what these two gain from lying about this fact, and whether you should hit "unsubscribe."

DON'T TRUST, ALWAYS VERIFY

A few years ago, my husband and I booked a room in a resort

for New Year's Eve. The reviews were fantastic and the photos incredible—we eagerly looked forward to our huge suite, view of a tropical beach, and pristine swimming pool. Unfortunately, reality didn't match the fantasy. Our actual room was a tin hut so small, we couldn't even reach the bed without climbing over a dresser first. At night we would hear all the beer bottles from the bar next door going into the dumpster on the other side of the wall from our room. Did I mention that on the far side (opposite the dumpster) there was a gas station, and the bedroom window was on the main hotel path? This was their "honeymoon suite."

The beach was two dumpsters away, and of course there was no view. And the beautiful pool? A small circle, surrounded by overgrown bushes and three deck chairs, housing a family of dead rats.

They charged us $800 per night.

"How on earth did this place get such good reviews?" I asked my husband. "It's such a scam!" It didn't take us long to get our answer. Within hours of posting our own—very honest, very disappointed—review, I got an email offering us a free five-night stay if I would take it down.

When I refused, they kept sweetening the deal until the honey turned to threats. Every review on that website was bought or browbeaten. I was—and still am—very angry thinking about all the people who were saving up for years to have a dream vacation, only to end up there. The review still stands, and I hope it saves even a few people from having the same experience we had.

We opened this chapter by watching a Get-Rich Guru lounge

against his telltale Lamborghini. Unfortunately, not all scammers have such obvious tells. Swindlers are finding stealthier methods of ripping us off than ever. Photos can be faked. Reviews can be fabricated. On platforms with little or no regulation (like TikTok), advertising is becoming so subtle it's nearly undetectable. Brands can promote themselves without even identifying as a business account. A business founder can create an account under their own name to promote their products (with content strategized and created by their professional team). So, is that a personal account or a business account? It's murky. With ads so seamlessly blended into our lives, we won't even notice we're being sold to.

The influencer you're following might not just be inauthentic. The account itself might be a fake. When an online creator starts to build an audience, scammers will come out of the woodwork to spoof their account. It's a type of identity theft, and even harder to stamp out than the financial kind. Many platforms offer "verified accounts," but it can be nearly impossible for ordinary content creators to get that blue check mark—those are often reserved for celebrities and those who can afford to pay for it.

It's happened to me more than once, especially on TikTok. A scammer will download my headshot, some of my videos, and create a new account that looks identical to my own—right down to using my NMLS number. If someone searches for me, they have no way of knowing whether they found the real me or a knockoff.

Here's the giveaway: the account starts messaging followers to offer services, and the links or products offered don't pass the smell test. I had one follower show me comment threads from one of these fake accounts. The scammer would say, "Do you need a loan? Let me give you a link to submit your information." Naturally, the link led to a site with no licensing information, for a so-called mortgage company that didn't really exist. It was a naked grab for people's personal and financial information. I report these people to the platform every time they pop up, but most of the time the platform does nothing. With TikTok in particular, I have reported at least four different accounts spoofing me, and they take no action at all. Even when a platform removes fake accounts, it doesn't stop the scammers from coming back and starting a new one.

So here's my last bit of advice for this chapter: When it comes to sniffing out scammers, become a detective. Assume every person you see online is trying to deceive you, and then only change your mind once you've thoroughly vetted their background and qualifications. If they want financial information, don't give an inch unless you can verify them three different ways. This will help you keep a clear mind as you attack our next chapter's goal: becoming a truly conscious consumer.

CHAPTER EIGHT

———

BECOMING A CONSCIOUS CONSUMER

Does any part of you still doubt that the money-driven internet has the ability to manipulate your mind? That it can, in a very real and direct way, shut off your brain's higher processing and render you functionally unconscious?

If you're still on the fence, consider this. In 2018, researchers at Princeton conducted a series of studies to measure how much we remember our experiences when we are documenting them on social media. What they found was that those who weren't using media to document their experience remembered far more about the event than those who curated it with images and posts. The paradox was not lost on the scientists: "Using media may prevent people from remembering the very events they are attempting to preserve."[156]

A lot of research has been conducted on how social media affects our memories, and the consensus seems to be that we are all suffering a bit from the "Google effect." This is when we don't bother to really learn or remember something because we know that we'll always be able to find the answer online.[157] When we're taking pictures on a hike, we simply don't put as much of that imagery into our biological brains because we know we'll have the photos to look back on. We're outsourcing our memories to our phones.[158]

Has social media affected your memory? Try this with me. Right now, put down this book, set a timer for thirty minutes, and then jump onto Facebook, Instagram, TikTok—whatever social media platform is your favorite. Scroll, look at photos, do whatever you usually do. Just don't turn this page until the timer goes off.

I mean it—do not turn the page. If you want to actually see this exercise in action, you cannot cheat.

I'll wait.

All right, has the timer gone off? Then shut off your device and turn the page again.

Now, without touching your device, **write down the last five images you saw on social media.**

Can you do it? Maybe you recalled two images, maybe three—but five? The act of scrolling through social media trains your brain to forget what it's seeing from moment to moment, which is partly why we feel compelled to continue scrolling. This, in turn, exposes us to more and more advertisements as we shuffle on through.

I have to admit, I'm not totally surprised to hear that social media can affect memory. I recently visited an aging specialist, who had me undergo testing on cognitive function and short-term and long-term memory. I was shown a variety of images for one second each and questioned afterward on whether I had seen a match. I failed miserably. Bear in mind that I'm only in my mid-forties and—unless everyone's been lying to me—show no signs of early-onset dementia. My ability to retain information on a short-term basis has simply dwindled faster than it should have, and my hunch is that it's down to the time I spend scrolling.

While digital devices can help us learn and connect with others, too much screen time delivers what scientists call "impoverished stimulation" to the brain. Our brains are always building new neural pathways and discarding unused old ones, and screen time is like junk-food nutrition for that process. According to researchers at Harvard Medical School, we need a variety of online and real-life experiences to truly stimulate our brains. In fact, boredom is a big part of that process. Boredom allows our minds to wander and our imaginations to expand.[159]

Some of our memory problems come from the memories not being stored properly in the first place. Russ Poldrack, a neuroscientist at Stanford University, has found that digital multitasking can send new information to the wrong part of the brain. Information normally goes into the hippocampus for memory processing and storage. But if we're watching a video on one computer screen while researching something on a second computer screen, our newfound knowledge can slide into the striatum area of the brain instead. That's where we store skills and procedures. Instead of making complex connections with the rest of our long-term memory in the hippocampus, this distracted learning is shallow and rigid. We lose the ability to think deeply about our new knowledge or experiences.[160]

Is this hit to our memory an *intended* side effect devised by evil, money-grubbing tech developers? I'm guessing not. But a better question might be, does it matter? Assuming you didn't cheat on the five-image test, you've just seen firsthand evidence that this technology tampers with the functioning of your brain. It reduces your ability to consciously consume the images in front of your face. And if you did cheat on our little exercise—if, for example, you grabbed a piece of paper and took notes on what you saw—this only proves my point all the more. If we want to become truly conscious consumers, we need to start interacting with our media like you just did: with full and directed intention.

If you've read the preceding chapters and aren't scared yet, you might as well quit reading now. There's nothing more I can say to convince you. But if you're feeling that lightning jolt of realization, it's time to take some action. This chapter is all about how to wake up your unconscious mind: how to spot your enemy, alter your mindset from *Now, Now, Now!* to be future-focused, and separate yourself from the digital landscape by recapturing your love for the real world.

RECOGNIZE THE ENEMY

After all our discussions of clickbait, brainhacking, scammers, and the rest, you might be looking at your credit card statements and beating your head against the wall, wondering, "How on earth did I fall for all this? Why am I so stupid?"

You're not stupid. You're not even weak. You're just up against a seriously powerful, insidious, and wide-reaching enemy. Remember, the salespeople aren't knocking on your door. They're inside your house. They know everything about you, can predict your next move, are always growing smarter—and they are severely underregulated.

I'm not prepared to name and shame individual companies in writing, but I recently came across a TikTok of a young woman exclaiming, "Oh my God, I was just thinking about refinancing, and I found a website that shops lender for me! When I went to their website, it listed a rate of one-point-seven percent. I didn't even have to run my Social Security number! They just automatically gave me a rate of one-point-seven! I am so thankful!"

Of course the TikTok video was an ad, but it was expertly filmed to fly under the radar—to look like your best friend Katie just got an impossibly great mortgage rate by using a "magical mortgage site." All those sites that compare lenders for you? Only lenders who pay to play are on there. They collect your data and pass it on as a "trigger lead." You are a product being sold to someone else.

As an expert in this field, I can tell you that this type of misleading advertising is illegal. So why does it continue? Volume.

In 2019, YouTube revealed in a press statement that there were more than five hundred hours of video uploaded every minute. That adds up to more than an entire human lifetime, with no breaks, uploaded every day. TikTok hasn't released similar statistics, but they have announced that they have one billion active users per month,[161] and 83 percent of their users have uploaded at least one video.[162] There is no way any group of moderators or governing bodies can adequately review that much content, much less enforce the law—and that's just two platforms of many.

So what am I asking you to do? Give up? Fall into despair? Dump your money onto the front lawn and light it on fire?

Of course not. When you know *how* you're getting brainhacked, you're a lot less likely to get brainhacked. It's like those old "secrets of magic, revealed!" shows, where magicians would perform their illusions with see-through walls and cabinets—without the deception and misdirection that usually keep audiences fooled. This is what we've been doing up to now—revealing the many tricks our online illusionists keep up their sleeves: pay-per-click advertising, data tracking, neuromarketing, hypertargeted ads, and so on, all backed by the most sophisticated developers, marketers, and artificial intelligence in the world. Along the way, I've handed you pieces of armor to block each attack—ad avoidance, notification blocking, twenty-four-hour purchase delays, and more.

Now I'm going to give you the most important weapon of all—a brand-new mindset.

LOOK TO THE FUTURE

Quick, name the last six things you ordered off of Amazon. If you're like me, you'll primarily remember items with the longest-term use, if only because they're likely the most expensive. For example, I recently invested in a red-light therapy kit. It's supposed to help with circulation, reduce inflammation, and have other health benefits. I was very intentional about that and did a lot of research, because it was a big investment. I think it will be useful in the long run.

We tend to overlook the smaller expenditures—not just because they're cheaper but because they often fulfill short-term wants. In my case, that would be my drawer full of random kitchen appliances and tools I will never use. We don't remember buying them because we never truly needed them to begin with—they were, in fact, the result of our dopamine-fueled search for instant gratification. Those little purchases add up quickly, and can often eclipse the cost of the larger and well-considered items.

So what do we learn from this disparity between the purchases we remember and those we don't? There is a big difference between making a purchase to serve a momentary whim and a purchase to serve a long-term goal—and this is the heart of my first piece of advice: to best ignore the siren call of the short-term dopamine hit, focus squarely on your long-term future.

BRING YOUR FUTURE IN FOCUS

The dopamine-fueled internet is designed to turn your mind to mush, so let's take some time to whip it back into shape. I've curated for you a few exercises and self-regulation tips designed to help you avoid instant gratification by adopting a longer view.

EXERCISE 1: PICTURE YOUR FUTURE

As I've already mentioned, we Americans tend to veer sharply toward the "live fast, die young" approach, often failing to save for our financial futures. In 2021, I spoke to nearly three thousand people wanting to take out a mortgage loan. Frankly, a large number of retirees are letting their optimistic bias get the better of them when it comes to retirement and setting their house budget.

We mentioned in Chapter Four that the average American doesn't have enough retirement savings, and that means lower income in retirement. Unfortunately, many people want to sell their home when they're getting ready to retire, and they look around for their next house in a price range based on their *current* income. They haven't thought through the major change in lifestyle and finances they're going to face once they retire.

(NOT SO) FUN FACT

Median income, where half the incomes are higher and half are lower, gives us the most realistic picture of retirement incomes across the board.

So what was the median retirement income in 2022? A mere $46,360, down from $56,632 three years earlier. Retirement income tends to start a bit higher and fall as retirees get older. For example, the median income for households aged sixty-five to sixty-nine is $57,992, and the median for households older than seventy-five is $36,925.[163]

According to the Boston College Center for Retirement Research, half of today's US households will have insufficient retirement income to sustain their standard of living. Fidelity Investments estimates that most people will need 55 percent to 80 percent of their preretirement annual income after they leave their jobs and stop working. Their actual amounts depend on their lifestyle, expenses, and healthcare costs. The rule of thumb is that Americans in their sixties should have saved eight to ten times their annual salary for their retirement. So, if you're making $75,000 a year, you should have about $600,000 to $750,000 in your retirement account by the age of 67.[164]

But most people have far less than that. According to the Federal Reserve, the average person between sixty-five and sixty-nine has only $206,819.35 in the bank.[165] About one in three workers has a pension. The median annual pay-out they can expect is $9,262 for private pensions, $22,172 for state or local pensions, and $30,061 for federal pensions. Two-thirds of US workers say they are confident that they've saved enough, but the Employee Benefit Research Institute discovered that less than half of those workers have actually sat down to calculate their retirement needs.[166] Since millions of people won't have enough money, more than half say they'll continue working in retirement.[167]

So how do you want your future to look? World travel and a paid-off home, or Netflix and ramen noodles, with a side of part-time job?

Start with a budget of your current expenses (I like Mint.com for that). Take a moment to look at your income versus expenses today, and dial into being fully accountable to your current financial situation. Are you saving money? What (if anything) could you cut? Once you fully understand your current situation, start thinking about and planning for retirement. Many investment companies like Fidelity or T. Rowe Price have calculators you can use to figure out the savings and investment levels you'll need.

Next time you go onto social media, set a timer. Remember that money journal we started using back in Chapter Three? For every minute you spend scrolling, bank another minute for writing in that journal, visualizing your own financial future. Doing so will not only rip you out of the unconsciousness of Scrollsville, but it will also make you think twice about getting onto social media in the first place. Because who wants to spend all their free time journaling? But if you take the time to visualize your future, do the math, and figure out how to achieve your dreams, you'll have a much better chance of ending up with the lifestyle you really want.

EXERCISE 2: FOLLOW YOUR MONEY

Now that you've clearly outlined your financial goals, it's time to use that information to help you enter the internet world with focus and intention. How often do you spend money that would be better put toward that fantastic vision of the future? Let's find out where your spending habits might be betraying you.

Remember the money journal and budgeting steps I recommended in Chapter Three? Let's get even more granular. For thirty days (or, if you want some serious brownie points, ninety days), track all of your expenditures—not just your online spending, but everything. If you're not saving for retirement but spend hundreds (or even tens) of dollars on Instagram or Amazon junk every month, that's a problem you can fix. Judging by the average American's retirement income, you're going to *need* that $100 later, more than you *want* that second black sweater now. So repeat after me: "Nothing is more important than my future. There is nothing on the internet I need." As you conduct this exercise, remember to check your spending history for unnecessary recurring subscriptions and other lingering unconscious buys.

We've talked about reviewing your subscriptions several times so far. In case you haven't noticed, turning products into subscription services is a long-term trend in our economy. It's all based on the "razor-and-blades" business model that was developed in the early twentieth century. Sell the customer a razor handle, even at a loss, and you'll keep them coming back for blades. Many products with refills have used this model over the years for long-term profits, from Swiffers to printer ink cartridges.

Subscriptions take it to the next level: you can have the product for the list price (which may not be cheap at all), but it won't actually work unless you pay for a subscription. Your brand-new BMW with heated seats? You pay for your warm bootie by the month. Your fancy exercise bike? Without the subscription to the workout plan, it works just like a budget model. All kinds of apps and services now entice you into this model, and you're likely to keep paying for the services long after you stop using them.

A quick note: Obviously, I think this exercise is well worth the time, but bear in mind that all these apps have their flaws. Like everything else these days, Mint.com is a PPC-driven app, and it will constantly refer you to specific advertisers trying to sell you loans or credit card offers. Just recognize those ads for what they are, and ignore them. Ironically, there's even a subscription service that promises to automatically unsubscribe you from other subscription services. The TrueBill app (owned by Rocket) offers to identify all your recurring subscriptions and help you unsubscribe. Whether that will actually save you time and money in the long run is for you to decide.

EXERCISE 3: KEEP THAT FUTURE VISION FRESH

As you transition your mindset toward the long view, do whatever you can to make impulse buys distinctly uncomfortable. Since we've already got our money journals open, let's go ahead and add a couple new items to our "justify this purchase" questionnaire:

- How long do you think this purchase will give you value?
- What are you trying to accomplish with this purchase?

With the last question in particular, consider your motivation for buying. Does this purchase fulfill a short-term want or a long-term need? For example, if you're spending extra on designer brands because you hope it will help you fit in socially, this is likely a short-term want.

What about the motivation of fear? Sometimes at 2:00 a.m., I imagine I'm a great cook. Other times, I imagine I'm going to somehow cook my way out of Doomsday. When I doomscroll and feed my anxiety with a pattern of frequent monitoring, I buy survival gear. I have seed kits guaranteed fresh for a hundred years. I've got an oven downstairs that will let me bake with hot rocks. Do I know how to use any of this stuff? Absolutely not. Do I think it's really going to be useful in any way? Not in daylight, I don't. I'm trying to buy my way out of a problem that isn't fixable with money. And the reality is that overspending on fixes for imaginary problems makes your real present and your real future worse.

On the other hand, perhaps you dream of better health, higher education, sharper professional skills, or a small business of your own. These are positive aspirations. Working on them now is good for you, now and later. Making a realistic plan toward those goals and spending money (carefully) to support them will serve you much better over time.

That said, always approach each purchase with care. If you buy a subscription to a fitness app that you will never use, it's still money down the drain. By reviewing your purchases, you may find that **resolving your feelings is a better use of your time than clicking a buy button.** You can't buy a feeling of belonging, nor a better marriage. You can't buy a perfect life, so save your money and invest in your relationships with time, communication, and commitment. They're priceless.

LIVE IN THE PRESENT

While we keep the future in mind, we don't want to live there all the time. We need to stay grounded in the present moment so we can perceive and understand our situations—our feelings, choices, relationships, and experiences. Escapism can help us relax, as long as it's an occasional break for our imaginations to work. When we spend too much time disconnected from reality, we surrender to unconsciousness, and become all the more vulnerable to manipulation. I want to give you some practical steps to keep your feet on the ground, and build up safeguards for your points of vulnerability.

SET LIMITS

Earlier in his career, sociologist BJ Fogg developed much of the research and behavioral modeling that helped tech developers get us so deeply hooked on the abstract, remote world of the internet. In recent years, he has written a book and teaches courses on how to get unhooked from the technology impulse and spend cycle.

Since BJ's the expert here, let's borrow a tip from his book *Tiny Habits*, aimed at helping us regulate our own behaviors. Let's say our goal is to wean ourselves off the internet and focus more on our real-world lives. BJ recommends starting by putting a time restriction on your social media use every day—no more than sixty minutes on each platform. If you use several platforms—and most of us do—you're still allowing social media to take a huge chunk out of your day. But we all need to start somewhere.

Now check whether your apps of choice have time-restriction options. If so, set each app to block you out after your time limit has expired. I've personally tried this on TikTok, and I can't recommend it enough. To make sure I wouldn't lift my own restriction, I locked my settings using a completely random and unknown passcode—and I haven't lost myself in mindless scrolling since.

If cutting back your social media makes you feel like you're in withdrawal, with increased anxiety, sleeplessness, and restlessness, don't dismiss it. After all, you've been engaging in addictive behavior and you crave dopamine. Try going cold turkey for a week. As we covered in Chapter Five, the impulse to indulge will get more intense in an "extinction burst," and then fade away. Once you have broken that dopamine-reward cycle, you can gradually reintroduce some social media with time limits.

FREEZE YOUR CREDIT

One Thanksgiving, my sister received a call from Chase Bank indicating suspicious activity on her card. Someone was trying to use her information to buy a car in Southern California; my sister lives in Seattle. We still haven't unwound the mess of how they stole her identity, but she has taken steps to ensure it does not happen again.

Freezing your credit can be a great financial protection move in general, preventing strangers from impersonating you and destroying your financial life. But it can also prevent you from undermining your own finances. Say you're in unconscious-consumer mode, mindlessly scrolling through social media, when you see an ad with a tempting credit card offer. If you're already distracted and emotionally vulnerable, applying might seem easy, even smart. What a low interest rate! What great cash back options! But as with any financial decision, opening a credit card should be done with forethought and intention. If you freeze your credit, you prevent yourself from making unconscious, spur-of-the-moment decisions that can hurt you in the long term.

FIGHT TECH WITH TECH

This book might make it seem like I hate technology. I don't. I love it. Moreover, I honestly believe that for every trick the dopamine-driven beast uses to manipulate us, we can derive an antidote from the same science.

Is scrolling messing up your short-term memory like mine? Want to meet your goals more effectively? Take a look at Brain-Tap, an app designed to help you train your brain to reinforce positive habits through guided meditation. Keep in mind that BrainTap is a subscription-based app, so it'll require an ongoing investment. However, I've found it to be an investment worth making.

Part of the reason BrainTap works for me is that its creator, Dr. Patrick Porter, uses a technique called Dual Voice Processing to trigger the desired emotional and habitual response. And he does it in a way that really appeals to my snarkier side. I've always struggled with traditional meditation and motivation techniques. Unremitting support and positivity just generate an automatic "Yeah, right!" in my head. But Dr. Porter is, shall we say, not unremittingly positive.

Essentially, when I put on my headset, I hear Dr. Porter's voice saying, "You want to eat fresh, vibrant foods," to which I immediately want to respond with, "No, I don't!" laced with a string of expletives. But then he follows up with, "Smart people don't eat bad foods—they eat healthy foods that help them live longer. Are you a *smart* person? What would I say about you to others?"

You wouldn't think mockery or goading would help a person recalibrate her eating habits, but my fruit-and-veggies bowl overfloweth.

RECLAIM YOUR TIME

There's no doubt that developing a long-term, goal-driven per-spective can return control of your financial life to your own hands. But what about your personal life? Cutting back on your shopping and social media pursuits might feel like breaking up with a significant other—all of a sudden, you have a huge gap in your day that used to be occupied with tapping and scrolling. How do you deal with that gap before all those bad habits come crashing back in to fill the void?

My approach? Relearn to think like a kid. Here's another quick exercise. Take thirty minutes with your journal to consider a few questions: What were you like as a kid? What excited you back then? What intrigued you? If you could've done anything on a Saturday afternoon, what would it have been?

And now, the kicker: what can you do to resurrect that interest?

TOUCH GRASS

Part of relearning to enjoy the present moment and think like a kid, is to *go outside*. Leave your phone in your pocket or your car, and do something physical in natural light and fresh air. What doctors call "green time," i.e., being outdoors—particularly doing moderate activity outdoors—has a wealth of scientifically proven benefits for your brain, and for your outlook on life. Spending time in nature improves your memory and is associated with reduced symptoms of depression, anxiety, inflammation, and attention-deficit hyperactivity disorder. One study found that spending even five minutes in nature increases positive emotions and decreases negative ones.[168]

I recently took up surfing as a way to separate myself from my devices. Not to fully escape social media—that's not realistic—but to gain some balance in my day. At the time, I was finding myself running back to the computer far too often to check my stats: views, followers, comments, and the rest of those dopamine lures. "My God," I thought, "I have to get a life."

So I booked myself some lessons—then nearly canceled about fifteen times. The thing about being an adult is that we're far too good at focusing on what's difficult or uncomfortable. When you're a kid, you see a surfer or ice skater or mountain climber and think, "Oooh, I want to do that!" Then you jump in with both feet. As an adult, I looked out at the Northern California ocean and thought, "Who wants to step into that water? It's cold and full of sharks! My arm's going to get chewed off, and I won't even notice because of all the frostbite."

Spoiler alert—surfing is awesome. You can't bring a phone in the water, so it's truly the only place I can totally escape. It's just you and the ocean, and the ocean is a nonstop challenge. You have to stay focused because if you aren't paying attention to the pace of the ocean, you could get hurt. I spent most of my time learning to surf by wiping out and getting "washing-machined" by the waves. There's nothing like a good old salt slap in the face to bring you back to reality and keep you humble. I've had thrilling interactions with seals and dolphins, and one not-so-fun day, a shark. And bonus, after the initial investment of some lessons, a surfboard, and a wetsuit, it's about as cheap a hobby as you can get. As of this moment I still suck, and the outlook is grim. But you know what? That's okay! I still feel great every time I get out of the water.

I've also started walking four or five miles a day outside, with no podcast or music—just me and my thoughts. It's a great anxiety killer. I'm calmer and more balanced all day. As a bonus, I often use the app StepBet, which lets me win money for completing walking challenges.

Maybe you loved biking as a kid, but now when you think about going for a ride, all you can picture are the downsides. "All those road bikes and spandex are expensive. I'd be the slowest rider on the road. And besides, I am out of shape, it's dangerous—I could get hurt." Stop it. First of all, you don't have to invest in a professional bike or join competitive racing just because you're an adult. You can buy a used bike off Facebook Marketplace, or just borrow your kid's ten-speed, and ride off into the sunset. Worried that you are too out of shape? Electric bikes are amazing! You can pedal and then use the motor when you're tired. And third, we all just survived COVID-19. We've spent years in and out of quarantine, having to treat the whole universe like a viral threat. Why fear steep hills when we can get wiped out by going to the grocery store? More to the point, why choose the internet over the ocean when there are just as many sharks online?

I'm not sure when we as a society let ourselves get brainwashed into believing scrolling, shopping, and consuming were the only fun things to do. But at the end of the day, the thrills we get off social media are temporary, artificial, and in the long term, often damaging to our personal and financial well-being. So right now, grab that journal. Remember what used to get you excited about life. Then get out there—outside your house—and embrace it.

GET UP AND GO

We started this chapter with yet another exercise illustrating how easily our online usage can make us disconnect mentally and become unconscious consumers. Whether you realize it or not, you're being pressured to sleepwalk through your own life. Consider this your wake-up call!

The PPC-fueled beast might have fed off your financial lifeblood until now, but technology can just as easily be used for your good. There are dozens of resources out there—apps, YouTube channels, and more—designed to help you recalibrate your thinking and reclaim control of your future. Hundreds of professionals in a host of fields have found themselves exactly where I am, eager to pull back the curtain on the tricksters manipulating society. Use our resources to help open your eyes, retrain your brain, and invest yourself in pastimes that liberate and empower you, not addict and exploit you.

And stay tuned for our next chapter, where we discuss even greater opportunities for seeing good—and doing good—thanks to the internet.

CHAPTER NINE

USING OUR INTERNET POWERS FOR GOOD

In November 2021, a sixteen-year-old kidnap victim from North Carolina was rescued two states away after she alerted passersby with a simple, three-step gesture: she showed her open hand, folded her thumb to her palm, and then folded her fingers over her thumb. This gesture was publicized internationally in 2020 through a media push by the Canadian Women's Foundation as a silent signal for help (particularly for those housebound during the pandemic). A passing motorist recognized the sign, called 911, and followed the car giving mile markers to the police until they caught up. The sheriff's office of Laurel County, Kentucky, told the media that this signal likely saved the girl's life. And how did this young girl and her rescuers learn about it? It was popularized on TikTok.[169]

I've spent the majority of this book warning about the minefield that is social media, news media, and online advertising. By now, we know that we should enter that minefield only with intention, keeping our eyes open for traps that will lower our defenses, make us vulnerable to manipulation, and cause us to spend zombie money.

But this is not the internet's only side. As much as I highlight the negatives of the internet, it can be an incredibly positive place full of opportunities to improve ourselves, support our neighbors, aid great causes, and more. Yes, almost every corner of the internet was designed with the aim of taking our money—but if you truly enter with intent, you can use this technology to achieve some goals of your own.

Let's talk about how we can use our internet powers to protect and improve our own lives—not to mention the world at large—by spotlighting corruption, supporting worthy causes, getting involved with our communities, reverse engineering PPC ads, and using social media to its best advantage.

BRING LIGHT TO DARK PLACES

Recent years have seen a tidal wave of social activists and internet sleuths uncovering the shady dealings of powerful or ill-intentioned people. Turns out, it's harder to get away with behaving badly when anyone with a device can blow the whistle on you. Here's just a small sampling of online do-gooders who've worked to uncover or overcome injustice, most of them in the last few years.

#METOO

One of the most famous social media movements in history, #MeToo has fundamentally shifted public attitudes toward sexual harassment, and altered the power balance in the media industry (possibly forever). The movement really began in 2006, when activist Tarana Burke used the phrase to empower sexual assault survivors through solidarity. The phrase rose to national and international prominence as a Twitter hashtag in 2017, when actress Alyssa Milano used it in conjunction with the allegations against movie producer Harvey Weinstein, and other stars like Gwyneth Paltrow, Jennifer Lawrence, and Uma Thurman followed suit. This movement really opened up people's eyes to what many women go through on a daily basis, and gave women the courage to speak up when they're treated badly.

INTERNET SLEUTHS

Bellingcat is a collective of mostly-volunteer online detectives organized in 2014 by founder Eliot Higgins. Using open sources on the internet like social media posts, free GPS maps, and other publicly available data, these investigators track down minute pieces of detailed evidence to expose and build criminal cases against perpetrators of hate crimes, war crimes, terrorism, and extremism. They have collaborated with journalists, human rights groups, and enforcement agencies around the globe.

Some of Bellingcat's high-profile cases include the poisoning of Russian and British double-agent Sergei Skripal, the downing of Malaysian Airlines Flight 17 (MH-17) by Russian missiles, and Syrian leader Bashar Al-Assad's use of chemical weapons on his own people. For example, in the case of MH-17, investigators tracked Facebook posts by members of the Russian military who transported the missile launcher used in the attack. Not only were they able to identify individuals by their profiles, but they traced specific vehicles and weapons by unique markings, down to dents and scratches in the paint.[170]

Eliot Higgins has written a book about his work, *We Are Bellingcat*.[171]

UNMASKING THE VILLAINS

In 2021, an anonymous group calling themselves The Great Londini became famous on TikTok for tracking down and exposing hateful internet trolls. This group of ex-military service members with surveillance experience started with about twenty members and grew to over six hundred. One of the founders, known only as "Leo," was inspired to pursue cyberbullies when his teenaged son committed suicide as a result of online harassment.[172]

The Great Londini find racist, violent, harassing, or otherwise offensive videos or comments, track down the owners of the accounts, and expose them to the relevant authorities. For criminal harassment, that might mean sending evidence to law enforcement. For others, it might mean having a viral video made about them or information sent to their employer. For children and tweens (the majority of offenders), it means contacting their parents. It is ironic (and weirdly satisfying) that the same tech that enables stalking and harassment can be used to put a stop to it.

HOOTERS, HANDBALL, AND HOTPANTS

In October 2021, female Hooters employees took to social media to protest a newly required piece in their uniforms: ultraskimpy bottoms that looked, to many, more like underwear than actual shorts. Within days, such a firestorm had arisen around the issue on social media that the CEO released a statement allowing employees to choose which bottoms they'd prefer to wear.

This echoed a protest in the summer of the same year, when the Norwegian women's beach volleyball team (known as beach handball outside the US) protested the league requirement that they play in bikinis. Since men's teams are allowed to play in tank tops and bike shorts, the women's team decided to compete in the same uniforms—and were promptly fined by the league. Viral video statements drew support from sports icons like Billie Jean King and celebrities like the musician Pink (who offered to personally pay the fines).

A petition to the league on Change.org drew more than sixty thousand signatures. The sports ministers of Iceland, Norway, Finland, Sweden, and Denmark published an open letter to the league urging them to review their outdated requirements. After three and a half months of public pressure, the International Handball Federation officially changed its uniform requirements to allow women players to dress like athletes instead of swimsuit models.

These events perfectly encapsulate why social media can be such a force for good. The people complaining about unfair or inappropriate treatment have, historically, never gotten anywhere by complaining to the very people who are treating them unfairly. Pressure from outside creates change, and social media has the power to amplify individual voices, and create that pressure in the right direction.

Public awareness and group action can also amplify good causes and get more people involved. Let's look at a few notable examples from recent years.

GOOD CAUSES, BIG AND SMALL

In 2014, the viral Ice Bucket Challenge raised $115 million for research into the degenerative disease amyotrophic lateral sclerosis (ALS). This outpouring increased the funding of the ALS Foundation by 187 percent.[173] It was one of the first viral challenges for a good cause, and it made huge waves. Social media can bring together people all over the world and leverage their goodwill to do amazing things. Not only can causes raise awareness, but they can get the word out about donor-matching opportunities.

To me, there's no greater antidote to getting stuck in an online rabbit hole than getting involved with your real-world community. Whatever your preferred platform, try to connect with people in your own neighborhood, and then look for opportunities to serve and support where you can. Here are some examples of people doing just that.

WORST TO BEST BIRTHDAY

Local news in Toledo, Ohio, reported in the fall of 2021 that a worried mother in a nearby small town posted to the neighborhood Facebook group that none of her six-year-old son's classmates RSVP'ed for his birthday party. So she invited the whole town. Word spread, and on the day of the party, most of the town showed up, including the local firemen. You'll find many such stories in the news, and it's a beautiful thing when a community rallies to bring joy to one of their own.

ANIMAL RESCUE—LITERALLY

After devastating hurricanes, floods, and other natural disasters, people evacuated by first responders are often told they must leave their pets behind. In other cases, people become separated from their pets in the chaos of the event itself. Volunteer groups and organized charities like Greater Good Charities, the Suncoast Animal League in Florida, and Operation Kindness in Texas undertake the effort to evacuate animals in advance of a crisis, rescue stranded pets, and reunite them with their owners.

These groups rely on social media to raise support, recruit volunteers, make connections with shelters and foster homes, and locate owners. The ability of social media to have wide reach, but also allow for individual responses, make it a valuable tool in these efforts.

Then again, maybe "community do-gooder" isn't really your style. Maybe you're more the avenging-angel type. If so, this next method might allow you to vent your righteous rage in a constructive way.

TURN THE ALGORITHM INSIDE OUT

Okay, this is where I admit to being a bit of a troll.

My father and grandfather were both in the navy. As a child, I used to sit at my grandfather's knee and ask what it was like to serve in World War II. Of course, he never had any real answers for me. He'd just sit there with a glass of gin and stare into my naïve little face until I stopped asking.

"Okay, Jennifer," you might be thinking, "what does this story have to do with being a troll?" Well, there are thousands of mortgage lenders out there eager to take advantage of veterans just like my father and grandfather. And that enrages me to no end.

Here's how it works. Veterans Administration (or VA) loans have the biggest profit margins for lenders. VA clients are also the most trusting and the least likely to shop around. When I first came into the business, it was widely known that the individual lenders who made the most money did government loans. They could get away with charging whatever they wanted, because they would tell the client that the VA sets the rates. The client would accept it, since it made sense that the government would set the rates on federally insured loans.

Let me be crystal clear: **This is a lie.** A massive, ugly lie—the banks and individual lenders set their own rates. They were blatantly lying to veterans so they could make more money. I still to this day can see the same borrower get quoted interest rates as much as 1.5 percent higher based on the lender they talk to—for the same exact loan.

You can see how this might rub me the wrong way. So here's where the trolling comes in. When I despise a particular company (and want to make my ad feed less tempting), I hit two birds with one stone by reverse engineering my PPC ads to take money out of their pockets. It's a fantastic strategy that you can use too.

What do I mean by reverse engineer? It's simple. Companies track your online movements so they can tailor their ads to your searches, right? Use this tool against them. Choose a company or cause you feel passionately about, then search for the keywords that enrage you the most.

If, say, you're into animal rights, Google "fur coat" and watch your screen fill with ads for fur and leather goods. There is simply no way you're going to spend money on those products—but every time you click, *their sponsors will pay*. You can watch their PPC dollars go down the drain, laughing all the way.

The main benefit to this approach is that every time you see one of these ads, your righteous rage will grow a little stronger. This can have two positive effects: 1) it'll annoy you into abandoning social media, which can only improve your life, and, 2) it'll spur you on to even stronger, more directed action. In my case, I decided years ago that I will only retire from mortgage lending when veterans are known as the most aggressive rate shoppers. I want lenders to flinch when vets show up at their door, because they know those vets come armed with sharp eyes and high expectations.

There is nothing that brings me more delight than clicking on a shady lender's ad. I love spending their money. Since I click on all the ads, I have the latest and greatest scams delivered to me by the algorithm. Every time I discover some new unethical lending or advertising practice, I make a video and post it to my YouTube channel. I use the bad guys' own advertisements against them, educating and warning potential borrowers—veterans like my father and grandfather—against their unscrupulous ways. Best of all, the lenders are paying to feed me the content I'm shaming them with.

In short, I am a troll—and you can be too. Simply identify your enemy, waste their advertising dollars, and then use your burgeoning anger to achieve some further good.

By the way, never forget that the change you achieve doesn't need to be global. As we explore in the next section, you can also use social media to protect your own physical welfare, broaden your worldview, and strengthen your financial life.

MAKE SOCIAL MEDIA WORK FOR YOU

In earlier chapters, we discussed how using social media without intent is like opening up your brain and wallet to manipulative advertisers. In fact, think of it like going to a shopping mall. If you're there to buy something for a specific event, you'll arrive with a plan of what you want to buy and how much you're willing to spend. But if you just wander in because you're bored, you could end up lugging out six bags of worthless junk, your mouth smeared with Jamba Juice and Cinnabon frosting. I agree, that sounds delicious, but it's probably not something you want to do often.

Protecting your wallet is a fantastic first step. But how can you take entering with intention to the next level? Let's look at how to approach major social media platforms mindfully, using each to its best advantage to protect yourself during crisis events, verify claims made by traditional news media, connect with your community, and more.

NAVIGATING CRISES

Social media—especially Twitter—can be an excellent vehicle for hyperlocalizing crisis events. If you feel an earthquake or hear about a wildfire (can you tell I live in California?), it's not going to do you a lot of good to check CNN for updates. Major news outlets are slow to respond to natural disasters, in part because it takes time to compile the necessary data and interviews into publishable stories. This is where Twitter can become invaluable.

Local residents will post updates much more quickly than media outlets, which will enable you to track which areas are hardest hit by the disaster, whether evacuations are being recommended, where evacuation points are being set up, and so forth.

Additionally, crisis events are often reported as occurring over an entire state or region, but the danger might vary within that area. Twitter can help you recognize your personal degree of danger. For example, my husband and I often find ourselves laughing over reports of legendary, life-altering storms rolling in—while we enjoy patio dining under a cloudless sky. Reports offered by major media outlets sometimes just don't reflect your local experience.

For a much darker example, let me take you back to the summer of 2020. There were people all over the political spectrum protesting in different parts of the country. I'm all for citizens exercising their First Amendment rights! It's a valid and necessary part of our democracy. But unfortunately, a big demonstration usually creates a big distraction for law enforcement. People with ill intent used the protests as a cover for violence, arson, looting, and mayhem.

We have a home in Manhattan, and at the time we were on lockdown at home in California. (I know that sounds very bougie, but stay with me.) I was trying to get as much information as possible about the neighborhood near our apartment, so we were watching the news reports nonstop. During that time, mainstream news coverage was so generalized that it was nearly useless. Most major outlets displayed only vague, nonspecific footage of storefronts, chaos, and police officers. Everything we saw was terrifying—fires in the street, stores being looted. I was afraid the apartment building would get stormed and set on fire, and people were going to get murdered.

Finally, I turned to social media to get live updates on what was happening on the ground, from people who were seeing it with their own eyes. Interestingly, it wasn't nearly as dramatic as the mainstream media portrayed it. On Twitter, you could follow individuals who were actively committing crimes and planning which stores to rob next with live, moment-by-moment videos.

There were tweets that said, "Gucci is next, grab a bat," with other people responding, "On my way," and "Get me something good!" On the one hand, it's pretty disturbing that anyone would be comfortable posting about criminal activity under their real name. On the other hand, it made me feel a lot more comfortable about my apartment, because the situation was more premeditated than chaotic.

Unfortunately, with the current state of society and media manipulation, I wouldn't be surprised if we soon see videos of violent riots popping up all over social media, only to later discover that they were staged and filmed a month in advance. But for now, if you can identify real people to follow, Twitter can be used to validate mainstream reports of crises as they unfold in real time.

GETTING THE FULL STORY

Generally speaking, I'd say that major media organizations still have the edge when it comes to accuracy in reporting. However, because their stories take longer to compile, they're often about twenty-four hours behind the curve. Worse, as we've seen before, they have an incentive to dramatize events to draw our clicks. So when a particularly controversial episode goes down, I recommend turning to social media to get a fuller picture of the story.

If an event is occurring five states away, traditional media gives you no way of verifying that their reports are accurate. Reading or watching people's firsthand experiences can give you greater detail and get you closer to the truth.

When Texas was hit by the 2021 snowstorm and infrastructure collapse, traditional media mostly provided general statistics, such as, "There are currently four hundred thousand people without running water," or "nine hundred fifty thousand people without electricity." We're desensitized to this type of reporting, because the 24/7 news cycle bombards us with bad news all day long. The reporters might as well be bobbleheads with voices like Charlie Brown's teacher: *wah wa wah.*

By contrast, it was TikTok that showed the real impact of that number. I recall a homeowner talking about how she'd recently bought her dream home, showing the pipes all frozen and broken, and her children packing their bags to evacuate. Users posted videos of themselves boiling snow to get any kind of drinking water, or burning their children's toys to stay warm. Knowing the full story galvanized internet users to put pressure on governmental organizations to take action. More importantly, seeing the human cost of these policy decisions gave us all a little of our humanity back.

MAKING OFFLINE CONNECTIONS

As far as I'm concerned, one of the best uses of Facebook—

because let's be honest, there aren't many great ones—is to join local groups. Many tend to focus on specific causes or organizations, which means they can be used to bring about deliberate, honed action. For example, as I mentioned in an earlier chapter, a Facebook group in my area banded together to help create and distribute PPE to local medical personnel during COVID-19. You might find other groups for less-dramatic but still worthy purposes, like volunteering in a community garden or supporting your local school's PTO.

Facebook groups can also be great for starting grassroots movements. Due to ongoing drought issues, the State of California ordered broad water-usage restrictions throughout my region, and the first place we heard about it was Facebook. Through another local Facebook group, I discovered that a developer planned to build three new hotels in our city, which would inevitably reduce general access to water even more. The public outcry didn't stop the hotels from being built, but they didn't threaten our water this year. So that's a step in the right direction.

Local groups on NextDoor or Facebook can also be a great way to save money and support your local community. You'll often find consignment sales, coupons, or offers to barter. Local businesses post sales and specials. Your public school district might have a "Spirit Night" fundraiser at your favorite pizza place, or a local charity might organize a dine-around party at upscale restaurants.

As a bonus, social media groups focused on local issues tend to be more civil than your average online comments section. After all, anything you post is linked to your actual name and picture, and frankly, there are social ramifications to being nasty to your neighbors. Meanwhile, because the group moderators can control who is allowed access, you're less likely to be overrun by trolls posting inflammatory content just to stir up trouble.

EXTENDING YOUR EDUCATION

I've mentioned this before, but it bears repeating: YouTube is incredible when it comes to free education. Hundreds of professionals at the top of their game share tips and knowledge freely, on every kind of topic from middle-school math, to building a business, to artistic skills, to political activism, to DIY guides. YouTube has saved me a fortune by teaching me to do things I would have paid someone else to do. When my refrigerator and water heater broke down, I found repair mechanics offering the exact advice I needed, down to the steps necessary to fix my specific branded machines.

FUN FACT

I have a client who is a tech engineer. Guess how he learned to code. YouTube.

I do all sorts of consumer education on my channels. For example, I did a video on the wonderful nonprofit Disabled American Veterans. I talked about how they help veterans work with the VA to get their disability ratings increased. The higher the rating, the more they get in monthly income. They can also receive additional benefits like property tax breaks. I have had countless veterans tell me that because of that video, they contacted DAV and got help. Now they have more income every month, which has substantially improved their lives. One little video can make a big difference. If you are a veteran, please check them out at www.dav.org.

As a reminder, always pay attention to how these educators or influencers are making their money. If they're asking you to go to a third-party site and input your credit card information, get out of there. If they're constantly trying to sell you on products you don't need, either skip their sponsor messages or find a different provider of information. There is so much great, informational content on YouTube, it's worth sifting through the scammers and fakes to find it.

CHECKING THE RECEIPTS

Social media is also a great way to cross-reference people to verify their identity, character, and experience. Assuming you have an online presence or own a business, potential employers and clients will want to know more about you, to tell if the persona you present is real. I've personally curated my Instagram page to match my business persona so people who find me on YouTube can verify that my identity and experience are authentic. I've already encouraged you to research online educators, sellers, and scammers to verify their credentials. Now it's time to flip that script. If it will benefit you professionally, use Instagram and other social media to enable others to verify you.

MINDFULNESS IS KEY

In all these areas—exposing problems, promoting good causes, restoring karmic balance, and gaining detailed knowledge, digital media can be used powerfully and well. That's especially true when the immediacy and intimacy of social media promote understanding and empathy. The common thread through them all is your own intentions and state of mind. Let's go over some practical steps for entering the internet with intent:

1. **Don't tie your self-esteem to social media.** Even if you're the kindest, most knowledgeable person in the world, there will always be at least twenty commenters saying you suck. You certainly should never take any comment about your appearance personally. Even supermodels get called "fat" and "ugly" on social media. Some people just love to bully others, which tends to get amplified online, because they believe no one will catch them. And on that note...

2. **Understand that anything you say, you may have to defend eventually.** You can tell a lot about someone by what they think is okay to post online. I personally know of a mortgage lender who put on a professional face at work, but as soon as she hit Twitter, it was all profanities and racial slurs. Is that who you want helping you through the biggest financial transaction of your life? I wouldn't. So make sure you only post things you'd be proud to say in front of your boss. Plenty of people have lost their jobs over things they posted on social media. The comedian Kevin Hart was disinvited from hosting the Oscars in 2019 over some ten-year-old tweets that he'd already apologized for. Nothing you post online ever really goes away.

3. **Consider the safety consequences of your posts.** This especially applies to younger people, who might not think twice about posting sexy photos or sharing their current locations. Most people who respond to their online activity with come-ons or threats of violence are all talk—but never forget that it's becoming easier and easier for bad guys to figure out

where you are. Between the geotagging we talked about in Chapter Five and the background-image searching that Bellingcat uses for good, stalkers and predators can be more invasive than you can imagine.

(NOT SO) FUN FACT

In 2019, the rising Japanese pop star Ena Matsuoka was sexually assaulted in her own home by an obsessive fan. He found out where she lived by studying her selfies. She was very careful never to show her home, even in the background. *He found her by zooming in on the train station reflected in her eyes.* He used Google Street View to identify the building, waited for her, and followed her home.[174] Think about that the next time you post your kid's first-day-of-school photos on the front steps of your house.

---

4. **Stop assuming your data doesn't matter.** Even if you don't mind cookies following you around the internet—which, frankly, you should—remember that your data is also being used to create profiles of people similar to you. Maybe I don't think anyone would be interested in a middle-aged mortgage lender from California, and maybe I'm confident that no one will be prying money out of my wallet anytime soon. But there are lots of women like me out there. I shouldn't be handing advertisers the tools they need to target them.

5. **If you own a business, be mindful of how you advertise.** Don't just think about dollars—think about how your ad impacts consumers. Are you pushing a message that can harm young viewers, such as promoting eating disorders, self-harm, or violence? You have every right to promote your business—but do it thoughtfully. Don't be part of the problem.

6. **Offset your internet hours with a useful pursuit.** Make a personal goal—to support a cause you love, improve your memory, improve the strength and flexibility of your body, or whatever feels important and compelling to you. For every hour you spend online, spend another hour working toward this positive, concrete goal. You'll be surprised how quickly you'll find joy and satisfaction outside the internet.

7. **Make your voice heard.** Guess who's on social media? Your senator and Congress member. Your governor. Your state legislators. The president. Now, they get a lot of messages all day long, and some of them aren't particularly kind or useful. But you have the opportunity to educate them, or even put pressure on them, to address the many serious issues we've covered in this book. The state of our world today *is not inevitable.* It's the result of many interlocking choices, and some of those choices are public policy that could be changed.

At the end of the day, all the advertising tools we've discussed so far in this book—social media, PPC ads, neuromarketing, hyper-targeting, and the rest—are morally neutral. It's all about who's using them and for what purpose. If you're not being conscious about your internet use, then you're being controlled. But if you enter the internet with intent, you can use each of those tools to support your vision for a better future. So take control of your data. Decide what causes, companies, and products are worthy of your attention. Then mind your wallet. Remember that the ultimate goal of all these services is to pry money out of your hands. Don't let them.

As we'll find in the next chapter, trusting our moral compasses will help us make one of the most important decisions of our generation: what the future of our world should look like.

CHAPTER TEN

CHOOSING THE WORLD OF THE FUTURE

I love traveling to New York City, but every time I visit, both the mainstream media and online sources would have me believe that if I stepped outside my door, I'd be in constant danger of being shot or stabbed for having the wrong *something*—the wrong gender, race, sexual orientation, political views, or level of wealth. That the city was just a Thunderdome of warring factions waiting to rip each other apart.

Surprise! That's not the case at all. Every time I walk through Washington Square Park, I see the same thing: old, young, black, brown, white, rich, poor—everyone is there. No one's yelling. No one's fighting. They're just enjoying a sunny day in the city, same as me.

Sure, as a nation we have our conflicts. There's no sense pretending otherwise. But in my experience, no matter how often we're told that our country is locked in some kind of civil war, I keep finding that the actual people in my actual communities are fundamentally good and kind. In neighborhoods across America, if a storm knocks a tree into your house, your neighbors are going to show up with a chainsaw and help clean up the mess.

My point is, the real world is better than the one the internet likes to show us. It's brighter, more hopeful, and more beautiful. But when we fail to interact with the world—when we get ourselves trapped in depressing, violent, or divisive internet bubbles instead—our worldviews begin to warp. We already know how those internet bubbles form—we build them ourselves, one click at a time. And we already know how to improve them—by clicking more positive, productive, and reliable content, retraining all those algorithms to feed us better information.

But I think we can take this one step further. Because ideally, we wouldn't have an internet bubble at all—we'd be out in the world, achieving our own goals. So for this chapter, I want to talk about how to recognize the bubbles we don't even realize we're inhabiting, and the dangers inherent in the massive bubble looming right on the horizon: the metaverse. And most importantly, the ways that these bubbles harm us financially, emotionally, and as a society.

IDENTIFY YOUR BUBBLE

I grew up in Corona Del Mar, California, a suburban beach town where just about everyone held the same set of values: eat healthy, exercise, go to college, marry "well," and make a lot of money. It wasn't diverse, and it wasn't always interesting, but it was peaceful in its own way. There were no protests, no civil unrest, and barely any street crime.

Despite its tranquility, the culture of Corona Del Mar was still damaging to its residents in several ways—it was unswervingly superficial and had very outdated ideas about women. Every aspect of a woman's value and purpose in life was defined by the male gaze. Everything in a girl's upbringing was focused on how to be attractive and get a man. Case in point: I vividly recall my friend's mom coaching us on how to laugh so it would sound pleasant, and having us practice in front of her for feedback. After all, no man wants to marry a wife with a "bad" laugh. I'm not kidding. It's not even funny.

I hit my preteen years during the Kate Moss era, a time when my town became an echo chamber of, "Be thin! Be thin! Be thin!" At a sleepover, the host's mom advised all of us to put mustard on our toast at breakfast, instead of butter—because mustard doesn't have any calories. In fifth grade, I remember a boy "helpfully" telling me I should stop drinking my Coke because I'd get cellulite. I was ten, maybe eleven years old. I didn't even know what cellulite was.

Prettiness was the bare minimum. As a teenager, I recall getting ready for a date at a friend's house. I was dressed in a T-shirt and jeans. When my friend's mom saw me, she gasped, "You can't go out like that! Here, wear this instead." And she handed me a super-tight, short dress and heels. I was fifteen.

At the time, that perspective seemed normal. It wasn't until I went to UC Santa Barbara that I realized not everyone in the world was obsessed with being thin or beautiful. I'd grown up in a bubble, a constricting little bubble that was warping the perspectives of its residents. And I had no idea.

This same bubble exists now on social media. The sexualization of young girls on social media is terrifying. The prevalence of photo filters has fueled a huge increase in demand for cosmetic surgery or procedures. There's even a new term for it: "Snapchat dysmorphia."[175] A 2019 study showed that the more people use social media, the more likely they are to consider plastic surgery.[176] A study in 2020 found a long-term rise in searches for specific cosmetic procedures among Facebook and Instagram users.[177]

I understand getting addicted to the way you look with filters—it's happened to me. When I'm filming short content and I don't want to bother putting on makeup, I'll use a filter instead. It's quick and easy. But every time I revert from the filter to reality, I feel like I'm switching between Snow White and the wicked witch handing her the apple. It's jarring. I've literally screamed at the shock of seeing my real face after acclimating to the filter. It's a horrible feeling, and so depressing. You see what you *could* look like, if only you had perfect skin, or if only you had no wrinkles. If only…

It doesn't take long to put you in a terrible headspace where you start wondering which procedures you need, just so you can avoid that awful shock. But filters are free. Fillers aren't. All this pressure leads people to spend money they don't have to chase an ideal that isn't even real. It also feeds the negative feedback loop of addictive clicking, approval-seeking, and impulsive spending.

The bubble of artificial beauty is just one example of a damaging cultural environment, and the power of social media makes it incredibly destructive to young, vulnerable people. Instagram has made headlines over and over for its failure to police pro-anorexia content and advertisements on its platform. This came to a head during a congressional hearing about Instagram's negative impact on children, especially young women, when it came to body image and self-harm. A report in the *Wall Street Journal* found that it has caused teens to develop eating disorders, an unhealthy view of their bodies, and depression.[178] "Instagram perpetuates the myth that our happiness and ability to be loved are dependent on external things: For girls, it's appearance, and for boys, it's financial success," body image researcher Lindsay Kite told the *Washington Post* in 2021.[179]

Revelations about Instagram come on the heels of other evidence that social media is affecting young women, causing more anxiety, depression, and self-harm. Figures from the US National Center for Health Statistics are alarming: Suicides among young women fifteen to nineteen increased 87 percent between 2007 and 2020. (As you'll recall, 2007 was Year One of the smartphone and social media era). Between 2000 and 2020, suicides among girls aged 10 to 14 more than tripled.[180] As former Facebook and Pinterest executive Tim Kendall said in the documentary *The Social Dilemma*, "These services are killing people and causing people to kill themselves."[181]

Remember back in Chapters Two and Three, where we talked about the mental health effects of brainhacking? Anxiety, depression, and despair are not just unintended side effects of algorithms that push negative content. The algorithm *uses* these negative emotions to drive behavior that makes them more money from clicks, and from impulsive spending. And that exploitation is killing people. Anorexia has one of the highest death rates of any mental illness (the opiate epidemic knocked it out of first place).[182] **Let me say it louder: marketers push content that makes people suicidal, and social media companies make money off it.**

Incidentally, as of the writing of this book, Instagram (owned by Meta, a.k.a. Facebook) has paid lip service to this concern with some public statements and an updated "Help" page, but has still done nothing to actually stop the promotion of eating disorders on its platform. Not a thing.

Many of these young Instagram users have no idea they're in a bubble. Like me, they've been caught in an echo chamber that tells them they have to look and act a certain way—and worse, that *everyone else is doing it*. They're fed filtered, glamorized images that in no way reflect the real world, yet shape their personal reality.

So here's my question: what bubble might you be living in without even realizing it? Pay attention to the types of marketing that appear on your screen. What are they trying to sell you?

Specifically, let's look at the bubble you're in about your finances. Is it a scarcity bubble? Have you been looking for ways to borrow money with bad credit or make a lot of money quickly? If so, you're likely to see ads for predatory lenders and the kinds of bottom-feeding schemes we talked about in Chapter Seven.

If instead, you were a rich investor, what types of things would you search for? Maybe "best bank rates for high-net-worth investors." If you were very careful with every dollar, you might search for frugal tips, like "healthy recipes on a budget" or "retirement savings calculator." Be that person, or rather, copy that person's search history. You'll wind up getting ads that remind you to save instead of shop. Whatever bubble you find yourself in, think about what activities built those walls around you, and then do the opposite.

DECONSTRUCT YOUR BUBBLE

Now, back in Chapter Two, we talked about using your clicks to retrain the algorithm to feed you more balanced content. Feel free to do that now—but only if you're determined to keep inhabiting an internet bubble. If you're ready to escape, then instead of merely improving the bubble you've developed, try prodding it to see if it pops. Start by accepting that the bubbles we build online *do not reflect reality*. They might contain small grains of truth, but the articles and ads that form them are designed to garner clicks and make some fat cat money.

Don't believe me? Time to put your bubble to the test. Frankly, PPC advertising can make the internet a difficult place to round out our perspectives, so my advice is to get out into the world, talk to your actual friends and neighbors, and see what they believe about your internet bubble. One of the things we as a society are losing most rapidly right now is empathy—the ability to see someone else's perspective. It's become all too easy to cherry-pick stories and facts that support our existing worldviews, rather than challenging and refining our beliefs. So instead of continuing to wade through the muck of the internet, get out there and ask some questions of your actual community. Is the world really as bad as your Reddit thread or Facebook group has been telling you? I'd bet not.

One final thought on this topic: no matter what bubble you've been living in, if it's keeping you constricted—filling you with fear, anger, or anxiety—rather than helping you achieve your goals, it's time to pop that sucker and get out. At the very least, that should give you some practice escaping—which you might very well need once the metaverse reaches its peak.

THE BIGGEST, BADDEST BUBBLE OF THEM ALL

How has the COVID-19 pandemic affected you mentally and emotionally? On December 7, 2021, the US Surgeon General released a statement warning parents, doctors, educators, and public health officials of the pandemic's devastating effects on the mental health of children, teens, and young adults. Twenty-five percent of young people experienced depression, and another 20 percent suffered from anxiety. There was a 4 percent increase in suicide attempts among boys, and a 51 percent increase in suicide attempts among girls.

Let that sink in: **a 51 percent increase in suicide attempts among girls.** The particular impact on girls and young women is attributed to their tendency to rely on personal social connections to process their feelings. Isolation and having to rely on social media as their only outlet was devastating for many.

Obviously, these statistics are disturbing. But they're all the worse when you realize they're likely just a preview of our future. Because now in its infancy is the most compelling, most damaging internet bubble the world has ever known: the Metaverse.

The term "metaverse" was coined by writer Neal Stephenson, in his 1992 sci-fi novel *Snow Crash*. The book describes a postapocalyptic future where people escape their bleak, deprived real lives by immersing themselves in a virtual online world. Today, the metaverse (with a small "m") already exists as a thriving platform for commerce and entertainment. There are a number of online virtual "worlds" in which users can interact, consume other media like movies, lectures, or concerts, and use real money to buy virtual goods. They are a combination of video game, chat room, livestream, and shopping site. Some of the better-known examples include the 2003 release of the multimedia platform *Second Life*, and the multiplayer games *Fortnite*, *World of Warcraft*, and *Roblox*.

The next iteration of the lowercase metaverse is the use of virtual reality and augmented reality equipment to interact with those digital worlds. This merging of two immersive technologies into an all-consuming alternate existence is being spearheaded by the company Meta's (formerly Facebook's) capital-M "Metaverse."

In a 2021 Facebook earnings call, Mark Zuckerberg talked about how his company would transition from being a social media company to being a "metaverse" company. The Metaverse, he said, is "a virtual environment where you can be present with people in digital spaces. (It's) an embodied internet that you're inside of rather than just looking at. We believe that this is going to be the successor to the mobile internet."[183] While Zuckerberg presents his version of the Metaverse as a utopia, it is impossible to believe he could have missed the term's origin as a nightmarish dystopian prediction.

The Metaverse envisioned by Zuckerberg, who changed the name of his company to Meta, is a three-dimensional digital world whose components—storefronts, movie theaters, parks— are created by partnering companies staking out their corner of the virtual wilderness. The earliest versions of the internet gave us email and text-based communications. That has since made way for photos, videos, and livestreams. Now we're stepping into a 3-D representation of the internet, where you exist as an avatar that other users can see, you can virtually dress your avatar any way you want, and you can meet anyone you want anywhere you want—as long as you're wearing your virtual-reality headset.[184]

But what most future adopters don't understand is that the Metaverse hasn't been built for them. It's been built by and for advertisers. Remember all the methods marketers use to hack your brain? The Metaverse will be brainhacking on steroids—essentially, the ultimate unconscious-money extractor.

Let's think over a few ways they might try to pull that off.

THE LURE

Not long ago, I came across a really cool—and disturbing—piece of art: *The Future Looks Bright,* by the German artist Kunstrasen. It depicts a man in a sharp-looking suit, walking cheerfully off to work, briefcase in hand. All around him is a barren landscape full of dead trees, an overturned car, a nuclear waste barrel, and an animal skull. He doesn't seem to notice the devastation surrounding him; in fact, his view is entirely obstructed by a pair of huge goggles. Everything in the image is rendered in black and white except this man's lenses, which are lit by brilliant color. Whatever might be projected inside those goggles, that's all he perceives as real.

This dystopian future, reminiscent of the postapocalyptic digital escapism depicted in movies like *The Matrix* and novels like *Snow Crash* and *Ready Player One*, is pretty much how I envision the Metaverse—a virtual-reality wonderland that will let us ignore the problems plaguing our actual world.

So how is Meta—formerly Facebook—intending to rope us into joining this platform? According to Mark Zuckerberg's public statements, the core messaging around the Metaverse is that it'll be entertaining, it'll be free, and it'll be for everyone. Let's dig into these assertions just a bit.

It'll be entertaining. If I were to say to you, "Hey, you like movies. I'll let you watch as many movies as you want as long as you let me brainhack you ninety-five percent of the time," you'd tell me to jump off a bridge. This is precisely the same deal Meta is offering with the Metaverse—they're just not being nearly so open about it.

"Hey," they'll tell you, "we're hosting a concert for free! You want to come?" Of course you're going to say yes. Who doesn't want a free show? But the entire concert will just be an opportunity for Meta to gather data on your buying preferences—and by the time you realize you've been brainhacked, you won't have a leg to stand on. Meta already uses its terms and conditions (that nobody reads) to gain a semblance of consent to their data mining. It's a safe bet that their Metaverse invitations will work the same way so that in accepting their invite, you'll also have accepted their terms and conditions, giving them full access to whatever data they could collect. Still sound fun to you?

It'll be free. Way back in 1973, Richard Serra described television as a means of delivering eyeballs to advertisers with the now-famous line, "If something is free, you're the product." No company runs on altruism. The Metaverse won't be offering free entertainment for the benefit of mankind—it's because they know entertainment will lure consumers into their shopping wonderland faster than just about anything else.

Roblox already has two hundred million monthly active users playing hundreds of thousands of games, many of which are already sporting branded products and experiences.[185] Meta is pumping $10 billion into building the Metaverse, and Apple, Google, and Microsoft are all developing their own concepts around the idea. Companies are already buying "real estate" in the virtual world: Philipp Plein, a Swiss fashion company, recently plunked down $1.4 million to buy sixty-five parcels in Decentraland, a virtual world with about eight hundred thousand users.[186] These are not experimental forays. Brands like Warner Brothers, Hyundai, Coca-Cola, Anheuser-Busch, Sephora, Nike, and HBO are all investing in the new platform. The market will be huge. Advertisers are frothing at the mouth to exploit us in the Metaverse. Why else would they be spending tens of millions of dollars on real estate that doesn't actually exist? They know they'll make billions more once we've arrived, ripe for manipulation.

It'll be for everyone. In the real world, a Gucci handbag could cost over $2,000. Right now in the metaverse (specifically in *Roblox*), the same handbag costs twenty-five dollars in real money—and anyone can afford a twenty-five-dollar purse, right?

Except, of course, that your big Gucci score isn't real—none of this will be real. You'll be in a nothing world buying nothing products to impress people you won't even know. And where will your money go? Into the hands of the selfsame advertisers who've manipulated you since you walked in that virtual door. Let's consider how they might collect all the monitoring data they'll need to crunch in order to keep the Metaverse optimized (and make even more money from data brokering). I've got a few guesses.

THE TRAP

Advertisers already spend billions to get into our heads and predict our next moves. With the Metaverse, that's about to get a whole lot easier, more manipulative—and more invasive. Here are just a few ways that Metaverse technology will open up a whole new dimension of brainhacking. Bear in mind, every single one of these tech capabilities *already exists*, and some of them are already part of your everyday life.

Headsets. Virtual-reality headsets are marketed as the best way to immerse yourself in the Metaverse experience. First-generation VR headsets track your head movements so the landscape you're seeing moves appropriately, giving the illusion that you are inside a real space. What Meta doesn't talk about is that the next generation of VR headsets work by tracking your *eye* movements, and how those eye movements will make them and advertisers more money.

Eye-tracking VR already exists in high-end headsets for business applications, and it is supposed to deliver better image quality at lower bandwidth, along with more realistic movement. The next step is for eye tracking to become available for home use, from PlayStation, Apple, and Meta itself. Once it does, you'll have all the privacy concerns about your data being tracked and recorded (as we discussed in Chapter Five), on a whole new and even more invasive level.[187]

As we discussed in Chapter Five, neuromarketers use eye-tracking data to measure an ad's effectiveness by comparing the duration of your gaze and signs of emotional arousal, like pupil dilation.[188] With that VR headset connected to the internet and interfacing with the Meta Mothership, all your eye movements can be recorded and exploited. So Meta isn't just inviting us into their wonderland; they're asking us to gift wrap them some high-level data on how to best ensnare us with advertising.

To add insult to injury, if your employer ever decides to hold company meetings via the Metaverse—as Bill Gates predicts by 2025 or 2026—your boss could use this eye-tracking data to tell how well you're paying attention. Employers can already record our keystrokes and read our emails. Do we really want to give them an even more invasive form of control?

Heart rate and movement monitors. Virtual workouts already exist that interact with your wearable fitness monitors, like Peloton and Mirror. So do fitness spaces in the metaverse—like Nikeland on the *Roblox* platform, where you can run races, jump on trampolines, or go swimming. The technology uses the accelerometer in your smartphone to track and virtually mimic your movements.

Any bets on how long it will be before the two are joined together? It may well happen before this book goes to print. Sure, your heart rate data can be useful feedback during a workout. But do you know what else it will reveal? How your body reacts to stimuli such as faces, colors, music beats, and (of course) advertisements. Data, data, data, all gift wrapped for those marketers out there.

Glasses and contact lenses. I got a call from my father the other day. He said, "You're never going to believe this. I'm calling you on my sunglasses!" He was so excited about his new Ray-Bans that connected to his Facebook account. He told me all about how he could take pictures or video of whatever he was seeing, he could listen to music, and he could place and record all his calls.

I asked, "So you can just walk around filming people wherever you go? You don't see anything wrong with that?"

"Oh, it's just for fun," he said. "And there's a light that goes on when you're recording."

I couldn't believe my ears. My dad is a smart guy. He's a lawyer. He's represented huge corporations for decades, and it never occurred to him how easily this technology could be misused. We had a conversation. He read the consent agreement. Those sunglasses were quickly thrown in the trash.

Here's the thing: Filming people in public isn't a privacy issue (though a lot of parents might have a problem with covert videos of their kids on the playground—I sure do). But how about indoors? These glasses come with transition lenses, so you could walk right into your friend's house—or the locker room at the gym—with nobody the wiser.[189] The developers could argue that a light goes on when you film. How many people know to look for that light? Not me, not before this encounter. Would you?

Now, my dad isn't a creep. I'm sure you're not a creep either. But there's no creep test for people who could buy these glasses. And there's no telling who is buying that data on the other end.

Despite the commercial failure of Google Glass in 2013, augmented-reality eyewear (including contact lenses) is already on the market, from over a dozen companies including Lenovo, Brother, Epson, and Microsoft. Even more products are in the works. Besides recording audio, video, and making calls, "smart" eyewear offers image overlay (rather than full immersion) that enables people to take the Metaverse with them everywhere they go.

Like the businessman in *The Future Looks Bright*, we too can soon block out aspects of the world we simply don't like. Is your morning commute a bit boring? Throw in a few unicorns. Hate the color of your walls? Don't bother painting—just change your filter. Wish your town had fewer homeless people? Great, maybe the software will erase them. Why fix our problems when we can just blot them out?

Voice Commands. Facebook has already developed an AI "builder bot" that lets Metaverse inhabitants build entire landscapes by describing what they want to see—oceanside sand dunes, for instance, or tropical islands with some clouds and trees. You can add sounds. This is a digital assistant to make Siri look like a wind-up toy; it will remember conversations you had last week on a certain topic or even handle follow-up questions without growing confused. If you were already concerned about how Facebook understands and predicts your every move, wait until they get an AI-equipped personal assistant collecting your innermost thoughts and transmitting them back to the advertisers. I can't be the only person who is freaked out about this.[190]

Sound manipulation. The auditory illusion of binaural beats was discovered in 1839, when Heinrich Wilhelm Dove demonstrated that playing two tones of slightly different frequencies in each ear causes the brain to produce the illusion of a rhythmic beat. By the 1970s, researchers were using these beats to alter subjects' state of consciousness—to slow down brain waves, increase REM sleep, or ease the user into a trancelike state. Binaural beat playlists on YouTube or music streaming platforms collect millions of hits from users who want help to concentrate on their studies or drift off to sleep.

Personally, I have to wonder how long it will be before the Metaverse embeds this tech into its sound design. Every time you enter a virtual store, the song in the background could be interfering with your brain function, lowering your inhibitions, helping you hyperfocus and lose track of time, lulling you into staying (and shopping) longer—all in the name of enhancing your immersive experience, of course. Talk about unconscious consumption!

Fragrance and temperature add-ons. If you've ever visited a simulator ride at an amusement park, you've experienced a crude version of this type of sensory immersion. Does your house run on smart systems? Any chance you'd connect these to the Metaverse? It would enhance your experience. Imagine that you're walking on a Metaverse beach when your thermostat clicks on, feeling just like the hot sun. Then your air fresheners activate, and you smell a sea breeze. Sounds nice, right? All a ploy to addict you to the Metaverse experience so you'll never want to leave.

If you can't tell, all this data collection and sensory manipulation has me spooked. We all freaked out when Edward Snowden revealed how deeply the NSA invades our privacy. But they're just reading our emails and listening to our calls, not tracking our eye movements and pulse to see what kind of ads we react to best. They're not trying to manipulate us into spending our money or abandoning our lives, like voodoo dolls responding to every pinprick. The NSA might be spying on us, but the Metaverse is trying to control us.

At this point, you might be thinking, "Jennifer, calm down and take off the tinfoil hat. I'd never fall for those addictive, 'immersive' ploys. And I'd definitely never agree to that much invasive data collection." But wouldn't you? According to a 2017 study by Deloitte, 91 percent of users hit "accept all terms and conditions" for apps and sites without ever bothering to read them, and for users between the ages of eighteen and thirty-four, it's as high as 97 percent.[191] Even if you did read them, it's not as if you can negotiate. If you need to update your phone, or your browser version, or any other utility, you have to accept the terms of service whether you like them or not. That conditions us to accept them for optional services too. What if the Metaverse comes with a four-hundred-page disclosure? Are you really going to read that to discover what types of data they intend to collect—from your very own body—before you hit "OK"?

The more data we offer these advertisers, the more adept they're going to become at appealing to every sense, shutting off every inhibition, and taking our money—and our free will—from our hands. The bubble of the Metaverse will simply harden around us like a steel dome, more impossible to escape every day. And when we opt in, we're just giving them the data they need to become that much stronger.

THE COMPANY YOU KEEP

You probably think you know the answer to this question already. "Easy," you might be saying, "I'll just meet up with my friends." And I'm sure you plan to. But will you truly be meeting new acquaintances and old friends, or will the Metaverse be crowded with imposters? It's a fair question. According to the Pew Research Center, about two-thirds of all tweets with links to popular websites are generated by bots and not humans.[192] How long before the Metaverse is teeming with advertiser-generated bots prowling around with offers to sell you something?

Will you be able to tell if the Metaverse character you're chatting with is real? In 2019, the FTC sued the dating app conglomerate Match Group for fraud. Match Group owns nearly every popular dating app: Match, Tinder, Hinge, OkCupid, and Plenty of Fish. The FTC alleged that Match was tricking customers into paying for a subscription by making them think bots and scammers were real love interests for them.[193] I wouldn't be surprised if the Metaverse launches the same way—populating the space with bots to make it look like the whole world has shown up to party. Why not? After all, Match got away with it—the court ruled that they were a "publisher," and therefore the fakes were not their fault.[194]

This can't have a positive effect on our social lives. Say you make a friend in the Metaverse who has some sudden life crisis and needs money. You have no way of knowing if that "friend" is a huckster or even human—it could be the bot version of the Nigerian prince scam. Or if we're talking romance, how will you know whether you're being catfished by pixels? And as those pixels keep you glued to your headset, all that Metaverse tech is reading your body data, exposing you to ever-more-targeted ads, and stealing your hard-earned money.

THE DARKEST TIMELINE

Picture a young man getting off his shift at a dead-end job, jumping into his car, and racing home to don his headset. The Metaverse, he believes, is where he truly lives—the only place he's ever felt special or achieved a goal. In the real world, he failed out of school years ago, lost his ambition, and is watching his health decline because he rarely thinks of eating well or exercising. Why should he? Health is irrelevant in the Metaverse. With his headset in place, he wants for nothing; he exists only to wander his imaginary world and buy imaginary products with his imaginary friends. In the Metaverse, he's a king. Why would he ever want to leave?

When you press him on the decision to live this way, he gets defensive: "Who are you to say what's real and what's not? At least here, I'm important. At least here, I matter."

Now imagine this young man is your friend, or nephew, or son.

Right now, we're making decisions that will shape the world for all future generations. Already, study after study reveals how damaging social media is for our teenagers. Not only does it distract them—in one study about half of the thirteen to seventeen-year-olds surveyed reported being on social media "almost constantly"—but it also disrupts their sleep, exposes them to bullying and rumors, and overall places them under tremendous peer pressure.[195] According to the Mayo Clinic, teens who frequently use social media—particularly at night—don't sleep well and suffer higher levels of anxiety and depression than counterparts who don't engage in social media as much. Those who have "an emotional investment" in social media— they might feel upset when prevented from checking their social media channels, for instance—are also more anxious and depressed and have trouble sleeping.[196]

Already, the effects of pervasive fear, grief and loss, school closures, quarantines, and other consequences of the COVID-19 pandemic have marked a generation of kids, making them feel isolated, anxious, and depressed, leading to increased suicide rates. And already, we're seeing signs that this will only get worse. Meanwhile, with in-person activities and jobs disappearing like smoke, people are going to be hard-pressed to find friendship or love, so all that isolation we experienced during COVID-19 will only increase tenfold.

To be fair, if you're still picturing the Metaverse with anticipation, you're not alone. I seriously doubt the average consumer is imagining their offspring rotting away as depressed, addicted Metaverse drones. No, they're just thinking, "Oooh, cool toy! Fun, new, now! What a great Christmas present for the kids!"

The thing is, humanity is often bad at thinking toward the future. A few years back, the lighthearted "debunking" show *Adam Ruins Everything* produced a piece on how paperless offices have actually worsened deforestation. Sounds counterintuitive, right? Turns out, a lot of dedicated forest land was being maintained and continually replanted for paper production. As soon as everyone went paperless, the demand for office paper dropped exponentially. Now the most profitable use for this commercial land is to scrape off the trees, lay asphalt, and erect buildings. A quick-growth forest was never going to be as good as an old-growth forest—but it was still millions of acres covered in trees. Now we have neither.[197]

So let's take a minute and think toward the future. We've already pictured how the Metaverse could destroy coming generations emotionally and socially, leaving them isolated, depressed, and purposeless. What other effects might we see—say, on the economy?

Imagine the Metaverse starts providing exciting "travel" opportunities, virtually transporting characters to destinations like the Grand Canyon, Great Wall of China, or Galapagos Islands. Some destinations depend on tourism for the health of their economies, so if that dries up, their businesses and towns could dry up as well. Natural areas like the Galapagos depend on tourism to fund their conservation efforts, so if your travel dollars disappear, so could a whole range of unique animal species. Hotels and airlines would suffer, meaning hundreds of thousands would lose their jobs.

Meanwhile, local mom-and-pop shops are already being forced out by online commerce, depriving the world of their uniqueness and specialization. My husband and I have felt privileged to travel a lot internationally, but on every trip, one depressing thing stood out to me. No matter if we were in France, England, Singapore, or Italy, I could barely find a local boutique to save my life. Everywhere, it was just Nike and Starbucks, the same as any mall in America. Not only did I feel like I was missing a chance to sample the flavor and individuality of each local culture, but I was disturbed to think of all the owners who'd lost their livelihoods. Online shopping is driving an entire job category into extinction: the entrepreneur who runs a small business to support their family. If these families don't even have the resources to run an online shop, how will they possibly compete against corporate giants for multimillion-dollar real estate in the Metaverse? We're going to wipe them out even faster.

With robots already taking over farm work, collecting our groceries, and delivering packages and pizzas, I sometimes worry that we'll soon "efficient" ourselves right out of civilization. Soon, the only jobs left will be as designers and developers supporting the Metaverse, or as scammers working those virtual streets.

These predictions might sound extreme. But to me, they're just the natural consequences of our current choices, the bubbles we're choosing to inhabit. All that free "fun" just isn't worth the cost of our money, time, and health—not to mention our children's futures.

JUST SAY NO

For starters, let's not even argue over how many minutes per day will be safe in the Metaverse. Zero is the best possible number. Do not sign up. Do not buy your loved ones those headsets. If your boss forces you to use the Metaverse for meetings, let them know you do so under protest, request to attend meetings sans headset, and refuse to invest any time or money into developing your avatar.

Maybe you're tempted by the financial opportunities available in the Metaverse. As a business owner myself, I get it—I could make a fortune by advertising there. But do I want to be part of the generation that destroyed society for my own benefit? Not on your life. Remember, no matter what lures you into the Metaverse, it won't be worth the cost: your own freedom and your children's future.

In short, stay as far away from this black hole as you can, emotionally and financially. The more we strap on our AI-driven VR goggles and block out these growing problems, the more we'll end up with a world none of us wants to live in.

That's the point, really. The Metaverse is just an individual product that demonstrates the direction we're headed. Like I said in Chapter One, the ability of tech companies to *buy and sell attention* has spawned every other intrusive, manipulative, distracting, addicting invention that came afterward. Brainhacking is now the way tech (and all the media that lives off of tech) earns its money. And human nature being what it is, anything that makes money is going to get more talent, more time, more effort, and more influence devoted to it.

Unless individuals (and hopefully, policymakers) take action, brainhacking is going to continue growing and becoming more insidious, in as many different forms as it can take. Whatever bubble you're living in, you need to get out sooner rather than later, because every iteration of technology is going to make it harder and harder to escape. So how can we begin popping those bubbles and staying grounded in reality? Let's spend our last pages considering some practical steps you can take to defend your dollars and your mind from the brainhackers of today and tomorrow.

CONCLUSION

I recently took a good look at the advertisements my devices were displaying and realized I was once again living in a bubble. In this version, everyone lives in beautiful houses filled with white furniture and little toy dogs, and all they think about is where they're going to vacation and how they're going to lose those last five pounds.

This isn't reality. It isn't even my reality. It's the escapist little dream world I've built with my internet searches, the dream that lets me pretend the problems in my life—or the world at large—aren't real. With all my research, awareness, and efforts, the bubble keeps closing in and I have to pop it over and over again.

This book is all about the enemies lurking in your own phone— those sneaky villains who want to lure you into unconscious spending. When Larry Page and Sergei Brin warned about the bias of the commercial internet back in 1998, they couldn't have fully foreseen how PPC-driven advertising would foster extremism and a divided society, nor how we as consumers would have to armor ourselves against the clickbait media, dopamine-fueled midnight spending sprees, brainhacking, and scammers that thrive in this environment. But then again, I'm certain it never crossed anyone's mind that we would turn all this mind-manipulating technology back on itself, using the internet to improve ourselves, our families, and our communities.

This push and pull is as old as invention itself. Innovators create unintended consequences. Those who see the inherent threats are decried as reactionaries, then sometimes later hailed as prophets. Mostly people find their way along a middle path, where they learn to harness the benefits and minimize the dangers. That's my hope for you.

Defending ourselves against digital manipulation isn't a one-and-done effort. It's also not a losing battle where we have to become Luddites to preserve our values. It's a constant practice of mindfulness, and a form of self-care.

As we wrap up this book, I want to offer some final pieces of advice aimed at protecting your time, attention, and life from the addictive, invasive lure of today's digital landscape: get comfortable with discomfort, and take every opportunity to reconnect with the real world.

EMBRACE DISCOMFORT

At this point in history, we as a species are basically babies using technology as a giant pacifier because we don't know how to self-soothe. People can't even stand in line at the grocery store without getting out their phones. We're too afraid we might accidentally make eye contact with someone, or worse, be forced to say hello. What you might not realize is that there's a true social and psychological benefit to discomfort. I don't mean "suffering is good for the soul"; that's a philosophical concept I don't want to touch.

I'm talking about what psychologists call "eustress." There is a certain amount of difficulty inherent to living a full life, and navigating these stresses is beneficial to us. We want things we don't have. We perceive problems and take action to change them. We stay attuned to all our feelings—good and bad—and receptive to the feelings of others. We try, fail, and learn.

Eustress forces us to grow and adapt, to expand our capacity to deal with the unexpected. Right now, tech is like a really terrible mother, one who's only too happy to shield us from the discomforts of the world—thereby stunting our growth—but who's also stealing our credit cards to run up a debt we never expected, and telling us terrifying bedtime stories to scare us and keep us close to her skirt.

If our phones are already enough to rob us of basic people skills, what will happen to our social lives when we depend on headsets that literally block out real people? Quit relying on technology to buffer you from discomfort. Go talk to people who think differently from you. Challenge your beliefs. Embrace the variety of thought, personality, and culture available when you set down your devices and look around.

Before we lose the basic necessity—and I'm talking Maslow's-hierarchy-of-needs level necessity—of human connection, let's agree to rupture our bubbles and embrace the real world.

PREPARE FOR REENTRY

If you truly want to protect your mind, money, and future generations, it's time to escape the digital world and run back to reality. Here are a few suggestions to get you started. Don't worry—I don't expect you to discard your devices, jump out your front door, and change your life all at once. Create tiny habits that build on each other. As Dr. Fogg reminds us, tiny habits stick better.

MOVE!

Consider weaning yourself off your tech addiction by distracting yourself with a short workout. Here's one tiny habit I've adopted: for every hour of my workday, I pause for five minutes of exercise. Doesn't sound like much, but you'd be surprised how challenging five minutes of arm circles or planks can be. I've lost close to ten pounds this way, and I can plank for five minutes straight.

(Okay, that's a lie, but the optimistic bias of my inferior frontal gyrus tells me I could get there by the time this book is published. Check out my YouTube channel to see if I really did: YouTube.com/c/JenniferBeeston.)

Meanwhile, my husband chose the tiny habit of walking our dog Muppet to the mailbox every day. It's just a half-mile down the street—not exactly a marathon. But what he discovered was that after a couple of weeks, he didn't want to stop at the mailbox. One day, he and Muppet headed down the street another half-mile to a coffee shop, then a little farther. Soon we had to have a little chat about boundaries, because Muppet is a tiny little Yorkshire terrier with short legs, and a three-mile walk was a bit much for her. The point is, even a few tiny habits can put you on a path to reconnecting with the real world. Mark and Muppet are now marathon walkers. They've made new friends all over town, and people stop their cars to say hello—mostly to Muppet.

CHANGE YOUR DEFAULT SETTING

Find a new backup plan for those moments when you're tired or bored so you don't reach for your phone. What's the most interesting, fulfilling thing you've done all month? My guess is that it had nothing to do with the internet. To prevent yourself from defaulting to the internet, make yourself a list of ten things you can do when boredom strikes. Here are some ideas to jumpstart your brainstorm session:

- **Dance in your kitchen like a little kid.** Why? Because it gets your body moving—and those happy hormones flowing. Every time I have a client who gets their offer accepted to buy a house, I do a celebratory dance on my Instagram story.

It's fun, the people who watch get to laugh at my terrible dancing, and we both get a mood boost!

- **Do a little work in the garden or yard.** Sunshine, vitamin D, and nature have all been shown to improve your mood. Plus, you'll have something satisfying to show for it.
- **Lean into your hobbies.** If you don't have any hobbies, just move. Muscle tone, bone density, and mobility only get more important as we age. So when your hips don't give out at age fifty-five, you'll thank me. Besides, it's a natural way to release dopamine—and you don't have to manipulate your own brain to get it!
- **Spend time with family.** If your house were on fire, what would you save? Not your phone. Not your virtual-reality headset. You'd save the piece of the world that means the most to you. So invest your time where your heart is, and hang out with the people you love.
- **Clean your house.** The exercise will do you good, and you'll be a lot more likely to interact with other humans if you're not embarrassed about having people over.
- **Read a book.** Expand your mind, learn something new, work on your memorization skills—or just spend some time exploring a world you have to visualize yourself, instead of being passively spoon-fed someone else's vision. It doesn't have to be a "hard" book. Personally, I love cozy mysteries about cooking. Nothing like a bake shop murder to get me relaxed! It's okay for books to be fun.
- **Create something.** Paint a picture. Paint a wall. Craft a birthday card. Whittle a stick. Just spend an hour putting something into the world that wasn't there before.
- **Appreciate tangible art.** Go to a museum, bookstore, library, or just an actual brick-and-mortar shop. Your fellow humans

like to create stuff. Make them feel like that matters to someone.

- **Call a friend.** Do you remember the last time a friend or family member just called you up because they felt like it? When it comes to getting a dopamine hit, a phone call's better than a social media notification any day.
- **Do service.** Mow a neighbor's lawn. Babysit a friend's kid. Help out at an animal shelter. Take items you no longer need to a local charity shop. Do something that reminds you that you aren't the center of the universe, no matter what your digital bubble might try to tell you.

Ultimately, if you can replace one session of scrolling with an activity that will improve your mind, body, family, or community, you can consider that a win.

STAY CONSCIOUS

You are now equipped to shut down unethical advertisers on sight. You have learned enough practical self-defense that you're empowered not to live in fear, but to use the internet safely and confidently as you grow your financial future.

Escaping the clutches of the internet is a social mission we can all get behind—so it's time to spread the word about unconscious consumption and face this battle together. If you want to know more about how tech can impact your wallet, check out my YouTube channel. If this book helped you, the first thing I want you to do is give it to someone else. Don't have it gather dust on a shelf. Spread the word. The more people who are prepared to fight clickbait, unconscious consumption, and the Metaverse, the better. We can remake the online world to serve humanity's best interests, instead of humanity serving the algorithm.

It's up to our generation to choose the world of tomorrow. Let's choose wisely.

APPENDIX

CHALLENGES AND ACTION ITEMS

CHAPTER ONE

Take the **UnHacking Challenge** to discover your hypnotic purchase patterns.

CHAPTER TWO

Take the seven-day **Reprogram Your Ads Challenge** to confuse the algorithm and make the ads you see less tempting.

CHAPTER THREE

Take the fourteen-day **Reboot Your Feed Challenge** to change the news you see. (Focus on the positive, not the negative.)

CHAPTER FOUR

Create friction to block unconscious purchases:

- Delete stored payment methods.
- Set up unbreakable rules.
- Keep a money journal.
- Cut the cord.
- Consider better ways to use your money.
- Picture the impact of your purchases.
- Slam the door on advertisers:
  - Ignore ads.
  - Unplug.
  - Unsubscribe.
  - Reply STOP.

CHAPTER FIVE

Stop playing the social media "slots":

- Turn off all your notifications—and I do mean all.
- Go onto social media only with intent.
- Do not gauge your worth by social media's attention.

CHAPTER SIX

Resist hypertargeting and data brokering:

- Refuse to give up your personal information for purchases without a clear privacy policy (and a compelling reason to do so).
- Use your phone settings at maximum privacy and opt out of location tracking, data collection, and ad customization whenever possible.

CHAPTER SEVEN

Spot the red flags of Gaslight Gurus:

- If their pitch features an expensive sports car, move on.
- If they're selling "secrets," don't listen.
- Do twenty minutes of Googling to discover their background.
- Follow the money.
- Look for outside verification of their skills.
- Double-check their assertions.

Ask questions about work-from-home kits:

- Are they really selling everything you'd need?
- Can someone in this field actually make this much money? If you were buying the ingredients of this kit separately, would it still cost this much?

Shields up against MLMs:

- Set a firm personal policy.
- Become spontaneously allergic.
- Hit mute.
- Deflect.

Spot the red flags on Influencers:

- Take the "guilty until proven innocent" approach.
- Watch for mathematical red flags.

CHAPTER EIGHT

Become a conscious consumer:

- Picture your future (plan for retirement).
- Follow your money (make a budget).
- Keep that future vision fresh in your mind.
- Set limits.
- Freeze your credit.
- Fight tech with tech.
- Reclaim your time.
- Touch grass.

CHAPTER NINE

Practice mindfulness online:

- Don't tie your self-esteem to social media.
- Understand that anything you say, you may have to defend eventually.
- Consider the safety consequences of your posts.
- Stop assuming your data doesn't matter.
- If you own a business, be mindful of how you advertise.
- Offset your internet hours with a useful pursuit.

CHAPTER TEN

Just say no to the Metaverse.

CONCLUSION

Change your default setting:

- Dance in your kitchen like a little kid.
- Do a little work in the garden or yard.
- Lean into your hobbies.

- Spend time with family.
- Clean your house.
- Read a book.
- Create something.
- Appreciate tangible art.
- Call a friend.
- Do service.

NOTES

1　Sergey Brin and Lawrence Page, "The Anatomy of a Large-Scale Hypertextual Web Search Engine," *Computer Networks and ISDN Systems* 30, no. 1–7 (April 1998): 124, https://doi.org/10.1016/S0169-7552(98)00110-X.

2　Mylene Mangalindan, "Yahoo Agrees to Acquire Overture For $1.63 Billion," *Wall Street Journal*, July 15, 2003, https://www.wsj.com/articles/SB105818965623153600.

3　Kylie Moore, "Google Advertising Statistics for 2021," *Digital Third Coast* (blog), accessed October 21, 2022, https://www.digitalthirdcoast.com/blog/google-ads-statistics.

4　Benjamin Mangold, "Google Ads Tutorial—How to Use Google Ads Step-by-Step," Loves Data, December 14, 2020, YouTube video, 51:38, https://www.youtube.com/watch?v=Cp22fC3v6o4.

5　Jon Simpson, "Finding Brand Success in the Digital World," Forbes Agency Council, *Forbes*, August 25, 2017, https://www.forbes.com/sites/forbesagencycouncil/2017/08/25/finding-brand-success-in-the-digital-world/.

6　"80 PPC Stats You Need to Know for 2022," WebFX, accessed October 21, 2022, https://www.webfx.com/ppc/statistics/.

7　Statista Research Department, "Digital Ad Revenue Share in the U.S. 2019 –2023, by Company," Statista, March 14, 2022, https://www.statista.com/statistics/242549/digital-ad-market-share-of-major-ad-selling-companies-in-the-us-by-revenue/.

8　Statista Research Department, "Google: Annual Advertising Revenue 2001–2021," Statista, December 2, 2022, https://www.statista.com/statistics/266249/advertising-revenue-of-google/.

9　"80 PPC Stats," WebFX.

10 Jordan Novet, "Amazon Has a $31 Billion a Year Advertising Business," CNBC, February 3, 2022, https://www.cnbc.com/2022/02/03/amazon-has-a-31-billion-a-year-advertising-business.html.

11 *Derren Brown: The Events*, episode 2, "How to Control the Nation," directed by Simon Dinsell, written by Derren Brown, Andy Nyman, and Iain Sharkey, featuring Derren Brown, aired September 18, 2009, on Channel 4.

12 Alice Pailhès and Gustav Kuhn, "Influencing Choices with Conversational Primes: How a Magic Trick Unconsciously Influences Card Choices," *PNAS* 117, no. 30 (July 13, 2020): 17675–79, https://doi.org/10.1073/pnas.2000682117.

13 Jefferson Online, "From ARPANET to World Wide Web: An Internet History Timeline," *Jefferson Online* (blog), November 22, 2016, https://online.jefferson.edu/business/internet-history-timeline/.

14 David Shedden, "Today in Media History: CompuServe and the First Online Newspapers," Poynter, September 24, 2014, https://www.poynter.org/reporting-editing/2014/today-in-media-history-compuserve-and-the-first-online-newspapers/.

15 Joe McCambley, "The First Ever Banner Ad: Why Did It Work So Well?," *Media Network Blog, Guardian*, December 12, 2013, https://www.theguardian.com/media-network/media-network-blog/2013/dec/12/first-ever-banner-ad-advertising.

16 Mark Nollinger, "America, Online!," *Wired*, September 1, 1995, https://www.wired.com/1995/09/aol-2/.

17 The Editors of Encyclopaedia Britannica, s.v. "Wi-Fi," in *Encyclopaedia Britannica Online*, last modified November 11, 2022, https://www.britannica.com/technology/Wi-Fi.

18 Claus Hetting, "How a 1998 Meeting with Steve Jobs Gave Birth to Wi-Fi," Wi-Fi Now, August 19, 2018, https://wifinowglobal.com/news-and-blog/how-a-meeting-with-steve-jobs-in-1998-gave-birth-to-wi-fi/.

19 Gary Rivlin, "Wallflower at the Web Party," *New York Times*, October 15, 2006, https://www.nytimes.com/2006/10/15/business/yourmoney/15friend.html.

20 "The Evolution of Social Media: How Did It Begin and Where Could It Go Next?," *Maryville Online* (blog), Maryville University, accessed December 6, 2022, https://online.maryville.edu/blog/evolution-social-media/.

21 Sarah Phillips, "A Brief History of Facebook," Technology, *Guardian*, July 25, 2007, https://www.theguardian.com/technology/2007/jul/25/media.newmedia.

22 Mark Hall, s.v. "Facebook," in *Encyclopaedia Britannica Online*, updated October 18, 2022, https://www.britannica.com/topic/Facebook.

23 The Editors of Encyclopaedia Britannica, s.v. "Twitter," in *Encyclopaedia Britannica Online*, last modified November 4, 2022, https://www.britannica.com/topic/Twitter.

24 Charles Arthur, "The History of Smartphones: Timeline," *Guardian*, January 24, 2012, https://www.theguardian.com/technology/2012/jan/24/smartphones-timeline.

25 Renee D. Goodwin et al., "Trends in Anxiety among Adults in the United States, 2008–2018: Rapid Increases among Young Adults," *Journal of Psychiatric Research* 130 (November 2020): 441–46, https://doi.org/10.1016/j.jpsychires.2020.08.014.

26 Matthew Jones, "The Complete History of Social Media: A Timeline of the Invention of Online Networking," History Cooperative, June 16, 2015, https://historycooperative.org/the-history-of-social-media/.

27 Hannah Ritchie and Max Roser, "Technology Adoption," Our World in Data, 2017, https://ourworldindata.org/technology-adoption.

28 Zi Chu et al., "Detecting Automation of Twitter Accounts: Are You a Human, Bot, or Cyborg?," *IEEE Transactions on Dependable and Secure Computing* 9, no. 6 (November–December 2012): 811–24, https://doi.org/10.1109/TDSC.2012.75.

29 "Mobile Fact Sheet," Pew Research Center, April 7, 2021, https://www.pewresearch.org/internet/fact-sheet/mobile/.

30 Stephen J. Blumberg and Julian V. Luke, *Wireless Substitution: Early Release of Estimates from the National Health Interview Survey, July–December 2016*, National Health Interview Survey Early Release Program (Hyattsville, MD: National Center for Health Statistics, May 2017), https://www.cdc.gov/nchs/data/nhis/earlyrelease/wireless201705.pdf.

31 Dipayan Ghosh and Ben Scott, "Facebook's New Controversy Shows How Easily Online Political Ads Can Manipulate You," *TIME*, March 19, 2018, https://time.com/5197255/facebook-cambridge-analytica-donald-trump-ads-data/; Giorgia Guglielmi, "The Next-Generation Bots Interfering with the US Election," *Nature*, October 28, 2020, https://www.nature.com/articles/d41586-020-03034-5.

32 "Mobile Fact Sheet," Pew Research Center.

33 Goodwin et al., "Trends in Anxiety."

34 Brooke E. Wagner et al., "Recreational Screen Time Behaviors During the COVID-19 Pandemic in the U.S.: A Mixed-Methods Study among a Diverse Population-Based Sample of Emerging Adults," *International Journal of Environmental Research and Public Health* 18, no. 9 (May 2021): 4613, https://doi.org/10.3390%2Fijerph18094613.

35 Mark Beech, "COVID-19 Pushes Up Internet Use 70% and Streaming More Than 12%, First Figures Reveal," *Forbes*, March 25, 2020, https://www.forbes.com/sites/markbeech/2020/03/25/covid-19-pushes-up-internet-use-70-streaming-more-than-12-first-figures-reveal/?sh=5125f22d3104.

36 World Health Organization, "COVID-19 Pandemic Triggers 25% Increase in Prevalence of Anxiety and Depression Worldwide," news release, March 2, 2022, https://www.who.int/news/item/02-03-2022-covid-19-pandemic-triggers-25-increase-in-prevalence-of-anxiety-and-depression-worldwide.

37 "Internet Uptake Has Accelerated During the Pandemic," International Telecommunication Union, accessed December 9, 2022, https://www.itu.int/itu-d/reports/statistics/2021/11/15/internet-use/.

38 Meta, "Introducing Meta: A Social Technology Company," news release, October 28, 2021, https://about. fb.com/news/2021/10/facebook-company-is-now-meta/.

39 Luis Carretié et al., "Emotion, Attention, and the 'Negativity Bias,' Studied through Event-Related Politics," *International Journal of Psychophysiology* 41, no. 1 (May 2001): 75–85, https://doi.org/10.1016/ S0167-8760(00)00195-1.

40 Elizabeth Grieco, "Fast Facts about the Newspaper Industry's Financial Struggles as McClatchy Files for Bankruptcy," Pew Research Center, February 14, 2020, https://www.pewresearch.org/ fact-tank/2020/02/14/fast-facts-about-the-newspaper-industrys-financial-struggles/.

41 Joseph Lichterman, "Here are 6 Reasons Why Newspapers Have Dropped Their Paywalls," Nieman Lab, July 20, 2016, https://www.niemanlab.org/2016/07/ here-are-6-reasons-why-newspapers-have-dropped-their-paywalls/.

42 Goodwin et al., "Trends in Anxiety."

43 World Health Organization, "COVID-19 Pandemic Triggers."

44 Jessica Mahone and Philip Napoli, "Hundreds of Hyperpartisan Sites Are Masquerading as Local News. This Map Shows if There's One Near You," Nieman Lab, July 13, 2020, https://www.niemanlab. org/2020/07/hundreds-of-hyperpartisan-sites-are-masquerading-as-local-news-this-map-shows-if-theres-one-near-you/.

45 Brendan Nyhan, "Americans Trust Local News. That Belief Is Being Exploited," *New York Times*, October 31, 2019, https://www.nytimes.com/2019/10/31/upshot/fake-local-news.html.

46 Dan Kennedy, "Exposing the '"Pink Slime" Journalism' of Journatic," *Media Nation* (blog), July 5, 2012, https://dankennedy.net/2012/07/05/exposing-pink-slime-journalism/.

47 Indira A. R. Lakshmanan, "Finally Some Good News: Trust in News Is Up, Especially for Local Media," Poynter, August 22, 2018, https://www.poynter.org/ethics-trust/2018/ finally-some-good-news-trust-in-news-is-up-especially-for-local-media/.

48 Utpal Dholakia, "How Anxiety Affects Our Buying Behaviors," *Psychology Today*, March 3, 2020, https://www.psychologytoday.com/us/blog/the-science-behind-behavior/202003/ how-anxiety-affects-our-buying-behaviors.

49 BJ Fogg, *Tiny Habits: The Small Changes That Change Everything* (New York: Mariner Books, 2020).

50 "Transcript: The Beat with Ari Melber, 12/15/21," MSNBC, December 15, 2021, https://www.msnbc.com/ transcripts/transcript-beat-ari-melber-12-15-21-n1286516.

51 Robin Blades, "Protecting the Brain against Bad News," *Canadian Medical Association Journal* 193, no. 12 (March 22, 2021): E428–29, https://doi.org/10.1503/cmaj.1095928.

52 Roy H. Perlis et al., "Association Between Social Media Use and Self-Reported Symptoms of Depression in US Adults," *JAMA Network Open* 4, no. 11 (November 2021): e2136113, https://doi.org/10.1001%2Fjamanetworkopen.2021.36113.

53 K. C. Madhav, Shardulendra Prasad Sherchand, and Samendra Sherchan, "Association Between Screen Time and Depression among US Adults," *Preventive Medicine Reports* 8 (August 16, 2017): 67–71, https://doi.org/10.1016%2Fj.pmedr.2017.08.005.

54 Associated Press, "Starbucks, PepsiCo and More Brands Pull YouTube Ads in Growing Boycott," *Hollywood Reporter*, March 24, 2017, https://www.hollywoodreporter.com/news/general-news/starbucks-pepsico-more-brands-pull-youtube-ads-growing-boycott-988721/.

55 U.S. Financial Literacy and Education Commission, *U.S. National Strategy for Financial Literacy 2020* (Washington, D.C.: U.S. Financial Literacy and Education Commission, 2020), https://home.treasury.gov/system/files/136/US-National-Strategy-Financial-Literacy-2020.pdf.

56 Oscar Contreras and Joseph Bendix, *Financial Literacy in the United States* (Santa Monica, CA: Milken Institute, 2021), https://milkeninstitute.org/sites/default/files/2021-08/Financial%20Literacy%20in%20the%20United%20States.pdf.

57 Carmen Reinicke, "Education Secretary Miguel Cardona Says Personal Finance Lessons Should Start as Early as Possible," CNBC, October 13, 2021, https://www.cnbc.com/2021/10/13/education-secretary-says-personal-finance-lessons-should-start-early.html#:~:text=Currently%2C%20a%20personal%20finance%20education,for%20students%20to%20take%20it.

58 Shannon Doyne, "Should All Schools Teach Financial Literacy?," *New York Times*, April 20, 2021, https://www.nytimes.com/2021/04/20/learning/should-all-schools-teach-financial-literacy.html.

59 Ann Carrns, "Pandemic Helps Stir Interest in Teaching Financial Literacy," *New York Times*, April 2, 2021, https://www.nytimes.com/2021/04/02/your-money/financial-literacy-courses.html.

60 Blades, "Protecting the Brain."

61 Alexandra Maftei and Andrei Corneliu Holman, "Cyberchondria During the Coronavirus Pandemic: The Effects of Neuroticism and Optimism," *Frontiers in Psychology* 11 (2020): 567345, https://doi.org/10.3389%2Ffpsyg.2020.567345.

62 Zhang Yue et al., "Optimism and Survival: Health Behaviors as a Mediator—A Ten-Year Follow-Up Study of Chinese Elderly People," *BMC Public Health* 22 (April 6, 2022), https://doi.org/10.1186/s12889-022-13090-3.

63 Meng Shi and Tianjiao Du, "Associations of Emotional Intelligence and Gratitude with Empathy in Medical Students," *BMC Medical Education* 20 (April 17, 2020), https://doi.org/10.1186/s12909-020-02041-4.

64 Ian Brissette, Michael F. Scheier, and Charles S. Carver, "The Role of Optimism in Social Network Development, Coping, and Psychological Adjustment During a Life Transition," *Journal of Personality and Social Psychology* 82, no. 1 (2002): 102–11, https://doi.org/10.1037/0022-3514.82.1.102.

65   Rawan Tarawneh, "How Does the Internet Affect Brain Function?," The Ohio State University Wexner Medical Center, February 26, 2020, https://wexnermedical.osu.edu/blog/how-internet-affects-your-brain.

66   Kevin McSpadden, "You Now Have a Shorter Attention Span Than a Goldfish," *TIME*, May 14, 2015, https://time.com/3858309/attention-spans-goldfish/.

67   K. D. Vohs, "Making Choices Impairs Subsequent Self-Control: A Limited-Resource Account of Decision Making, Self-Regulation, and Active Initiative," *Journal of Personality and Social Psychology* 94, no. 5 (2008): 883–98, https://psycnet.apa.org/doi/10.1037/0022-3514.94.5.883.

68   Brian Wansink and Jeffery Sobal, "Mindless Eating: The 200 Daily Food Decisions We Overlook," *Environment and Behavior* 39, no. 1 (January 2007): 106–123, https://doi.org/10.1177%2F0013916506295573.

69   Philip W. Jackson, *Life in Classrooms: Reissued with a New Introduction* (New York: Teachers College Press, 1990), 149.

70   Dean Spears, "Economic Decision-Making in Poverty Depletes Behavioral Control," *CEPS Working Paper*, no. 213 (December 2010), https://gceps.princeton.edu/wp-content/uploads/2017/01/213spears.pdf.

71   "Blue Light Has a Dark Side," *Harvard Health Blog*, July 7, 2020, https://www.health.harvard.edu/staying-healthy/blue-light-has-a-dark-side.

72   Michael Breus, "Technology and Sleep," The Sleep Doctor, updated September 9, 2022, https://www.sleep.org/how-sleep-works/ways-technology-affects-sleep/.

73   Joanna A. Cooper, "Screens and Your Sleep: The Impact of Nighttime Use," Sutter Health, accessed June 7, 2022, https://www.sutterhealth.org/health/sleep/screens-and-your-sleep-the-impact-of-nighttime-use.

74   Dominique Mosbergen, "Here's Why America Is Dumping Its Trash in Poorer Countries," *Mother Jones*, March 9, 2019, https://www.motherjones.com/environment/2019/03/heres-why-america-is-dumping-its-trash-in-poorer-countries/.

75   Laura Parker, "China's Ban on Trash Imports Shifts Waste Crisis to Southeast Asia," *National Geographic*, November 16, 2018, https://www.nationalgeographic.com/environment/article/china-ban-plastic-trash-imports-shifts-waste-crisis-southeast-asia-malaysia.

76   Sophie Hares, "Global Waste Could Increase by 70% by 2050, According to the World Bank," World Economic Forum, September 25, 2018, https://www.weforum.org/agenda/2018/09/world-waste-could-grow-70-percent-as-cities-boom-warns-world-bank/.

77   *The True Cost*, directed by Andrew Morgan, produced by Life Is My Movie Entertainment Company and Untold Creative, 2015.

78   *Trashed*, directed by Candida Brady, produced by Blenheim Films, 2012.

79   Hope Cristol, "What Is Dopamine?," WebMD, last reviewed on June 14, 2021, https://www.webmd.com/mental-health/what-is-dopamine.

80 "Dopamine," Healthdirect, last reviewed April 2021, https://www.healthdirect.gov.au/dopamine#:~:text=Dopamine%20is%20responsible%20for%20allowing,of%20dopamine%20in%20the%20brain.

81 Trevor Haynes, "Dopamine, Smartphones & You: A Battle for Your Time," *Harvard University* (blog), May 1, 2018, https://sitn.hms.harvard.edu/flash/2018/dopamine-smartphones-battle-time/.

82 Haynes, "Dopamine, Smartphones & You."

83 Haynes, "Dopamine, Smartphones & You."

84 Anderson Cooper, "Transcript: What Is 'Brain Hacking'? Tech Insiders on Why You Should Care," *CBS News*, April 9, 2017, https://www.cbsnews.com/news/brain-hacking-tech-insiders-60-minutes/.

85 Cooper, "Transcript: What Is 'Brain Hacking'?"

86 Celeste Headlee, *Do Nothing: How to Break Away from Overworking, Overdoing, and Underliving* (New York: Harmony Books, 2020).

87 Marcelo Gleiser, "Does Technology Make You Freer?," NPR, October 21, 2015, https://www.npr.org/sections/13.7/2015/10/21/450473648/does-technology-make-you-freer.

88 Jason M. Watson and David L. Strayer, "Supertaskers: Profiles in Extraordinary Multitasking Ability," *Psychonomic Bulletin & Review* 17, no. 4 (August 2010): 479–85, https://doi.org/10.3758/pbr.17.4.479.

89 Gloria Mark, Victor M. Gonzalez, and Justin Harris, "No Task Left Behind?: Examining the Nature of Fragmented Work," *CHI 2005* (April 2005): 321–30, https://doi.org/10.1145/1054972.1055017.

90 Gloria Mark, Daniela Gudith, and Ulrich Klocke, "The Cost of Interrupted Work: More Speed and Stress," *CHI 2008* (April 2008): 107–110, https://doi.org/10.1145/1357054.1357072.

91 Abraham, "Technology Promised Us More Free Time, Have We Been Fooled?," Tech Smart, April 29, 2021, https://voonze.com/technology-promised-us-more-free-time-have-we-been-fooled/.

92 Paulina Villegas and Hannah Knowles, "Iceland Tested a 4-Day Workweek. Employees Were Productive—And Happier, Researchers Say," *Washington Post*, July 7, 2021, https://www.washingtonpost.com/business/2021/07/06/iceland-four-day-work-week/.

93 Anna North, "The Five-Day Workweek is Dead," Vox, July 13, 2021, https://www.vox.com/22568452/work-workweek-five-day-four-jobs-pandemic.

94 North, "The Five-Day Workweek is Dead."

95 Jennie Overton, "The Great Resignation Update: Limeade Employee Care Report," Limeade, accessed December 9, 2022, https://www.limeade.com/resources/resource-center/limeade-employee-care-report-the-great-resignation-update/?utm_source=newswire&utm_medium=press_release.

96   Roy Maurer, "Remote Employees Are Working Longer Than Before," SHRM, December 16, 2020, https://www.shrm.org/hr-today/news/hr-news/pages/remote-employees-are-working-longer-than-before.aspx.

97   Peter Isackson, "How Western Media Misunderstand Chinese Culture," Fair Observer, July 7, 2021, https://www.fairobserver.com/culture/peter-isackson-daily-devils-dictionary-western-media-chinese-economy-culture-work-ethic-news-22001/.

98   Amanda Lenhart, Monica Anderson, and Aaron Smith, "Chapter 4: Social Media and Romantic Relationships," in Teens, Technology and Romantic Relationships, Pew Research Center, October 1, 2015, https://www.pewresearch.org/internet/2015/10/01/social-media-and-romantic-relationships/.

99   "The Dangers of Social Media on Marriage and Family," Northcentral Insights and Stories (blog), Northcentral University, May 1, 2017, https://www.ncu.edu/blog/dangers-social-media-marriage-and-family#gref.

100 Gwendolyn Seidman, "How Facebook Affects Our Relationships," Psychology Today, May 28, 2015, https://snip.ly/15hlk#http://www.psychologytoday.com/blog/close-encounters/201505/how-facebook-affects-our-relationships.

101 Russel B. Clayton, Alexander Nagurney, and Jessica R. Smith, "Cheating, Breakup, and Divorce: Is Facebook Use to Blame?," Cyberpsychology, Behavior, and Social Networking 16, no. 10 (October 2013): 717–20, https://doi.org/10.1089/cyber.2012.0424.

102 Spencer Palmer Christensen, "Social Media Use and Its Impact on Relationships and Emotions" (master's thesis, Brigham Young University, 2018), https://scholarsarchive.byu.edu/etd/6927/.

103 Beth Levine, "Pornography Habit Is Linked to Erectile Dysfunction, Research Suggests," Everyday Health, July 22, 2020, https://www.everydayhealth.com/erectile-dysfunction/pornography-habit-is-linked-to-erectile-dysfunction-research-suggests/.

104 J. D. Power, "Alternative Lenders Satisfying Customers with Digital Platforms and Quick Approvals, But Still Not Viewed as Customer Driven, J. D. Power Finds," news release, March 24, 2019, https://www.jdpower.com/business/press-releases/2019-personal-loan-satisfaction-study.

105 Tom Anderson et al., "Consumer Lending: Understanding the Empowered Borrower," Experience Radar 2015, PwC, 2015, https://www.pwc.com/us/en/consumer-finance/assets/pwc-consumer-lending-radar.pdf.

106 Joana Coutinho de Sousa, Neuromarketing and Big Data Analytics for Strategic Consumer Engagement: Emerging Research and Opportunities (Hershey, PA: Business Science Reference, 2018).

107 Eben Harrell, "Neuromarketing: What You Need to Know," Harvard Business Review, January 23, 2019, https://hbr.org/2019/01/neuromarketing-what-you-need-to-know.

108 "How Neuromarketing Works: 5 Neuromarketing Techniques," MasterClass, updated November 2, 2021, https://www.masterclass.com/articles/neuromarketing-explained#5-neuromarketing-techniques-to-know.

109 Logan Chierotti, "Harvard Professor Says 95% of Purchasing Decisions are Subconscious," *Inc.*, March 16, 2018, https://www.inc.com/logan-chierotti/harvard-professor-says-95-of-purchasing-decisions-are-subconscious.html.

110 Will Leach, *Marketing to Mindstates: The Practical Guide to Applying Behavior Design to Research and Marketing* (Lioncrest Publishing, 2018).

111 Roger Dooley, "Marketing to Mindstates with Will Leach," January 23, 2020, in *Brainfluence*, podcast, 35:58, https://www.rogerdooley.com/will-leach-marketing-to-mindstates/.

112 Samuel M. McClure et al., "Neural Correlates of Behavioral Preference for Culturally Familiar Drinks," *Neuron* 44, no. 2 (October 14, 2004): 379–87, https://doi.org/10.1016/j.neuron.2004.09.019.

113 Ania G. Wieckowski, "When Neuromarketing Crosses the Line," *Harvard Business Review*, January 23, 2019, https://hbr.org/2019/01/when-neuromarketing-crosses-the-line.

114 *Secrets of the Superbrands*, directed by Adam Boome and James Vale, produced by BBC Productions (United Kingdom, 2011), television miniseries.

115 Charles Duhigg, "How Companies Learn Your Secrets," *New York Times*, February 16, 2012, https://www.nytimes.com/2012/02/19/magazine/shopping-habits.html.

116 Clare Stouffer, "Internet Tracking: How and Why We're Followed Online," *Norton* (blog), June 29, 2021, https://us.norton.com/internetsecurity-privacy-internet-tracking.html.

117 Matt Burgess, "Google Has a New Plan to Kill Cookies. People are Still Mad," *Wired*, January 27, 2022, https://www.wired.com/story/google-floc-cookies-chrome-topics.

118 "Tracker Market Share," WhoTracksMe, accessed December 14, 2022, https://whotracks.me/.

119 "Consumer Attitudes on Personalized Ads," Innovid, 2020, https://info.innovid.com/2020-consumer-attitudes.

120 Steven Melendez and Alex Pasternack, "Here Are the Data Brokers Quietly Buying and Selling Your Personal Information," *Fast Company*, March 2, 2019, https://www.fastcompany.com/90310803/here-are-the-data-brokers-quietly-buying-and-selling-your-personal-information.

121 *Global Customer Data Platform Market Size by Type (Cloud Based and On-Premises), by Application (Large Enterprises, and SMEs), by Geographic Scope and Forecast* (Lewes, DE: Verified Market Research, April 2022), https://www.verifiedmarketresearch.com/product/customer-data-platform-market/.

122 Jay Stanley, "Why Don't We Have More Privacy When We Use a Credit Card?," *ACLU* (blog), August 13, 2019, https://www.aclu.org/blog/privacy-technology/consumer-privacy/why-dont-we-have-more-privacy-when-we-use-credit-card#:~:text=Under%20GLB%2C%20companies%20can%20sell,when%20they%20fill%20out%20applications.

123 "Experian Revenue 2011-2022 | EXPGY," Macrotrends, accessed December 14, 2022, https://www.
     macrotrends.net/stocks/charts/EXPGY/experian/revenue#:~:text=Experian%20annual%20revenue%20
     for%202020,a%206.54%25%20increase%20from%202019.

124 "TransUnion Revenue 2011-2022 | TRU," Macrotrends, accessed December 14, 2022, https://www.
     macrotrends.net/stocks/charts/TRU/transunion/revenue#:~:text=TransUnion%20annual%20
     revenue%20for%202020,a%2014.63%25%20increase%20from%202018.

125 Equifax, "Equifax Delivers Record Revenue and Eighth Consecutive Quarter of Double-Digit Growth,"
     news release, February 9, 2022, https://investor.equifax.com/news-events/press-releases/detail/1214/
     equifax-delivers-record-revenue-and-eighth-consecutive.

126 Sarah Brady, "Loan Scams and Loans to Avoid," Debt.org, updated November 12, 2022, https://www.debt.
     org/credit/loans/loan-scams-to-avoid/.

127 Jennifer Valentino-DeVries, "Tracking Phones, Google Is a Dragnet for the Police," New York Times, April
     13, 2019, https://www.nytimes.com/interactive/2019/04/13/us/google-location-tracking-police.html.

128 National Gendarmerie, "[PREVENTION] Preserve your children! If you've been following Facebook,
     a post channel is all the rage right now," Facebook, February 23, 2016. https://www.facebook.com/
     gendarmerienationale/posts/1046288785435316.

129 Jess Staufenberg, "French Parents 'Could Face Prison' for Posting Photos of Their Children on Facebook,"
     The Independent, March 2, 2016, https://www.independent.co.uk/news/world/europe/french-parents-
     told-their-children-might-sue-them-for-pictures-put-on-facebook-a6906671.html.

130 "5 Reasons Not to Post About Your Child on Social Media," Jellies (blog), accessed December 14, 2022,
     https://jelliesapp.com/blog/5-reasons-not-to-post-about-your-child-on-social-media.

131 Debra Kamin, "What Goes on Behind the Cameras at Home Makeover Shows?," New York Times, May 27,
     2022, https://www.nytimes.com/2022/05/27/realestate/home-makeover-renovation-lawsuit.html.

132 Michelle Cyca, "What Happens When You Buy Instagram Followers," Hootsuite (blog), April 14, 2022,
     https://blog.hootsuite.com/buy-instagram-followers-experiment/.

133 Jeff Kauflin, "Why Jack Dorsey's First-Tweet NFT Plummeted 99% in Value in a
     Year," Forbes, April 14, 2022, https://www.forbes.com/sites/jeffkauflin/2022/04/14/
     why-jack-dorseys-first-tweet-nft-plummeted-99-in-value-in-a-year/?sh=5fcd1a2a65cb.

134 Reuters, "Man Who Paid $2.9m for NFT of Jack Dorsey's First Tweet Set to Lose Almost
     $2.9m," Guardian, April 14, 2022, https://www.theguardian.com/technology/2022/apr/14/
     twitter-nft-jack-dorsey-sina-estavi.

135 Jacob Kastrenakes, "Beeple Sold an NFT for $69 Million," The Verge, March 11, 2021, https://www.
     theverge.com/2021/3/11/22325054/beeple-christies-nft-sale-cost-everydays-69-million.

136 "Multi-Level Marketing Businesses and Pyramid Schemes," Federal Trade Commission Consumer Advice,
     May 2021, https://consumer.ftc.gov/articles/multi-level-marketing-businesses-pyramid-schemes.

137 Emily Stewart, "MLMs Might Not Be Able to Get Away with Their Shady Promises Any Longer," Vox, October 22, 2021, https://www.vox.com/the-goods/22732586/ ftc-mlm-rohit-chopra-business-opportunity-rule.

138 Jonathan Berr, "LuLaRoe's Business Is Booming, but Some Sellers Are Fuming," *CBS News*, March 2, 2017, https://www.cbsnews.com/news/lularoe-multi-level-marketing-women-clothing/.

139 Hayley Peterson, "LuLaRoe Is Refunding Everyone for Pants that Customers Say 'Rip like Wet Toilet Paper,'" *Insider*, April 25, 2017, https://www.businessinsider.com/ lularoe-refunds-customers-for-defective-leggings-2017-4.

140 Alden Wicker, "Multilevel-Marketing Companies like LuLaRoe Are Forcing People into Debt and Psychological Crisis," Quartz, August 6, 2017, https://qz.com/1039331/ mlms-like-avon-and-lularoe-are-sending-people-into-debt-and-psychological-crisis.

141 Ally Arcuri and Donna Sarkar, "The Truth about Beachbody," Health Digest, updated December 13, 2022, https://www.healthdigest.com/480585/the-truth-about-beachbody/.

142 Lauren Debter, "Inside Beachbody's Billion-Dollar Fat Burning Empire," *Forbes*, April 10, 2018, https:// www.forbes.com/sites/laurengensler/2018/04/10/beachbody-carl-daikeler-shakeology/?sh=1b54c6e67960.

143 Debter, "Inside Beachbody's Billion-Dollar Fat Burning Empire."

144 Gaby Del Valle, "Multilevel Marketing Companies Say They Can Make You Rich. Here's How Much 7 Sellers Actually Earned," Vox, October 15, 2018, https://www.vox.com/the-goods/2018/10/15/17971410/ lularoe-lipsense-amway-itworks-mary-kay-mlm-multilevel-marketing.

145 Jon M. Taylor, "Chapter 7: MLM's Abysmal Numbers," in *The Case (for and) against Multi-Level Marketing*, (Consumer Awareness Institute, 2011), https://www.ftc.gov/sites/default/files/documents/ public_comments/trade-regulation-rule-disclosure-requirements-and-prohibitions-concerning-business-opportunities-ftc.r511993-00008%C2%A0/00008-57281.pdf.

146 Sabrina Barr, "A Travel Blogger Responds to Critics Who Accuse Her of Poorly Photoshopping Her Vacation to Paris," *Insider*, December 21, 2018, https://www.businessinsider.com/ travel-blogger-altered-vacation-photos-instagram-2018-12.

147 Rebecca Husselbee, "Instagram Influencer's Fake Travel Pics Revealed when Followers Notice the Exact Same Cloud Pattern in All of Her Snaps," *The Sun*, August 30, 2019, https://www.thesun.co.uk/ news/9825798/instagram-influencers-fake-travel-pics-revealed-exact-same-cloud-pattern-snaps/.

148 Jonathan Crossfield, "Full Disclosure: The Murky World of Influencer Marketing," *Chief Content Officer*, November 2017, https://contentmarketinginstitute.com/cco-digital/april-2019/ influencer-marketing-non-disclosure/.

149 Madeline Buxton, "Most Top Celebs Violate Sponsorship Rules on Instagram—Here's Why That Matters," Refinery29, June 13, 2017, https://www.refinery29.com/en-us/2017/06/158839/ celebrity-instagram-endorsements-violate-ftc.

150   Rebecca Stewart, "93% Of Celebrity Influencers Don't Signpost Ads Correctly on Instagram," The Drum, June 13, 2017, https://www.thedrum.com/news/2017/06/13/93-celebrity-influencers-dont-signpost-ads-correctly-instagram.

151   Federal Trade Commission, "FTC Staff Reminds Influencers and Brands to Clearly Disclose Relationship," news release, April 19, 2017, https://www.ftc.gov/news-events/news/press-releases/2017/04/ftc-staff-reminds-influencers-brands-clearly-disclose-relationship.

152   Jacinda Santora, "Key Influencer Marketing Statistics You Need to Know for 2022," Influencer Marketing Hub, updated November 4, 2022, https://influencermarketinghub.com/influencer-marketing-statistics/.

153   Santora, "Key Influencer Marketing Statistics."

154   Taylor Lorenz, "Rising Instagram Stars Are Posting Fake Sponsored Content," *Atlantic*, December 18, 2018, https://www.theatlantic.com/technology/archive/2018/12/influencers-are-faking-brand-deals/578401/.

155   Samone Wheeler, "Dealbreakers: Why Influencers Say No to Sponsored Partnerships," *Influence* (blog), Medium, May 14, 2019, https://influence.bloglovin.com/dealbreakers-why-influencers-say-no-to-sponsored-partnerships-fb2e02c622bb.

156   Diana I. Tamir et al., "Media Usage Diminishes Memory for Experiences," *Journal of Experimental Social Psychology* 76 (May 2018): 161–68,https://collaborate.princeton.edu/en/publications/media-usage-diminishes-memory-for-experiences.

157   Andrew Gregory, "How Social Media Is Hurting Your Memory," *TIME*, May 8, 2018, https://time.com/5267710/social-media-hurts-memory/.

158   Daryl Austin, "To Remember the Moment, Try Taking Fewer Photos," NPR, August 5, 2021, https://www.npr.org/sections/health-shots/2021/08/05/1022041431/to-remember-the-moment-try-taking-fewer-photos.

159   Debra Bradley Ruder, "Screen Time and the Brain," Harvard Medical School News & Research, June 19, 2019, https://hms.harvard.edu/news/screen-time-brain.

160   Saga Briggs, "6 Ways Digital Media Impacts the Brain," InformED, September 12, 2016, https://www.opencolleges.edu.au/informed/features/5-ways-digital-media-impacts-brain/.

161   Jessica Bursztynsky, "TikTok Says 1 Billion People Use the App Each Month," CNBC, September 27, 2021, https://www.cnbc.com/2021/09/27/tiktok-reaches-1-billion-monthly-users.html.

162   "TikTok Statistics–Updated Nov. 2022," Wallaroo Media, updated November 20, 2022, https://wallaroomedia.com/blog/social-media/tiktok-statistics/.

163   Kathleen Coxwell, "Average Retirement Income 2022: How Do You Compare?," *NewRetirement* (blog), February 24, 2022, https://www.newretirement.com/retirement/average-retirement-income-2022-how-do-you-compare.

164 Moriah Costa, "What's the Median Retirement Savings by Age?," *Synchrony* (blog), updated September 21, 2022, https://www.synchronybank.com/blog/median-retirement-savings-by-age/.

165 PK, "American Retirement Savings by Age: Averages, Medians and Percentiles," DQYDJ, accessed December 14, 2022, https://dqydj.com/retirement-savings-by-age/.

166 Jessica Dickler, "For Most Americans, $1.7 Million Is the Magic Retirement Number," CNBC, July 7, 2019, https://www.cnbc.com/2019/07/05/how-much-money-do-you-need-to-retire.html.

167 Coxwell, "Average Retirement Income 2022."

168 Alexa McRoberts, "The Importance of Spending Time in Nature," Thrive Global, January 21, 2020, https://thriveglobal.com/stories/the-importance-of-spending-time-in-nature/.

169 Jonathan Edwards, "A 16-Year-Old Girl Learned a Hand Gesture on TikTok to Signal for Help. Law Enforcement Says It Saved Her Life," *Washington Post*, November 8, 2021, https://www.washingtonpost.com/nation/2021/11/08/tik-tok-hand-sign-kidnapper/.

170 Terry Gross, "How Bellingcat's Online Sleuths Solve Global Crimes Using Open Source Info," in *Fresh Air*, NPR, radio, 35:36, March 2, 2021, https://www.npr.org/2021/03/02/972837924/how-bellingcats-online-sleuths-solve-global-crimes-using-open-source-info.

171 Eliot Higgins, *We Are Bellingcat: Global Crime, Online Sleuths, and the Bold Future of News* (New York: Bloomsbury Publishing, 2021).

172 Samantha Berlin, "Anonymous Vigilante Group Hunts Down Cyberbullies on TikTok," *Newsweek*, August 16, 2021, https://www.newsweek.com/anonymous-vigilante-group-hunts-down-cyberbullies-tiktok-1619795.

173 Chris Strub, "Ice Bucket Challenge Boosted ALS Association Annual Funding by 187%: Report," *Forbes*, June 11, 2019, https://www.forbes.com/sites/chrisstrub/2019/06/11/icebucketchallenge/?sh=4558c67c2411.

174 "Stalker 'Found Japanese Singer Through Reflection in Her Eyes,'" *BBC News*, October 10, 2019, https://www.bbc.com/news/world-asia-50000234.

175 Michael Reilly and Keon Parsa, "Social Media and the Rising Trend of Cosmetic Surgery," *Psychology Today*, September 17, 2019, https://www.psychologytoday.com/us/blog/dissecting-plastic-surgery/201909/social-media-and-the-rising-trend-cosmetic-surgery.

176 Jonlin Chen et al., "Association Between the Use of Social Media and Photograph Editing Applications, Self-Esteem, and Cosmetic Surgery Acceptance," *JAMA Facial Plastic Surgery* 21, no. 5 (September 19, 2019): 361–67, https://doi.org/10.1001/jamafacial.2019.0328.

177 Zachary H. Hopkins, Christopher Moreno, and Aaron M. Secrest, "Influence of Social Media on Cosmetic Procedure Interest," *Journal of Clinical and Aesthetic Dermatology* 13, no. 1 (January 2020): 28–31, https://www.ncbi.nlm.nih.gov/pmc/articles/PMC7028372/.

178 Georgia Wells, Jeff Horwitz, and Deepa Seetharaman, "Facebook Knows Instagram Is Toxic for Teen Girls, Company Documents Show," *Wall Street Journal*, September 14, 2021, https://www.wsj.com/articles/facebook-knows-instagram-is-toxic-for-teen-girls-company-documents-show-11631620739?mod=hp_lead_pos7.

179 Jennifer Breheny Wallace, "Instagram Is Even Worse Than We Thought for Kids. What Do We Do About It?," *Washington Post*, September 17, 2021, https://www.washingtonpost.com/lifestyle/2021/09/17/instagram-teens-parent-advice/.

180 Matthew F. Garnett, Sally C. Curtin, and Deborah M. Stone, *Suicide Mortality in the United States, 2000–2020, NCHS Data Brief,* no. 433 (National Center for Health Statistics, March 2022), https://www.cdc.gov/nchs/products/databriefs/db433.htm.

181 *The Social Dilemma,* directed by Jeff Orlowski-Yang, featuring Tristan Harris, produced by Larissa Rhodes, 2020.

182 Eric Graber, "Eating Disorders Are on the Rise," American Society for Nutrition, February 22, 2021, https://nutrition.org/eating-disorders-are-on-the-rise/.

183 Kyle Chayka, "Facebook Wants Us to Live in the Metaverse," *New Yorker*, August 5, 2021, https://www.newyorker.com/culture/infinite-scroll/facebook-wants-us-to-live-in-the-metaverse?source=search_google_dsa_paid&gclid=CjwKCAiA4KaRBhBdEiwAZi1zzmrTVvrAd_6J7IbSW9tR50tPN6Xoo0pqAzRuU6i55eNm_krhVI8emRoCfYUQAvD_BwE.

184 Shamani Joshi, "What Is the Metaverse? An Explanation for People Who Don't Get It," *VICE*, March 15, 2022, https://www.vice.com/en/article/93bmyv/what-is-the-metaverse-internet-technology-vr.

185 Ilyse Liffreing, "The Metaverse—How Brands Are Boldly Embracing Marketing's New Frontier," The Current, October 28, 2021, https://www.thetradedesk.com/us/news/the-metaverse-how-brands-are-boldly-embracing-marketings-new-frontier.

186 Asa Hiken, "Why Brands Are Buying Land in the Metaverse—and How They're Doing It," *Ad Age*, March 1, 2022, https://adage.com/article/digital-marketing-ad-tech-news/buying-virtual-land-metaverse-what-brands-need-know/2402851.

187 Scott Stein, "Watching Me, Watching You: How Eye Tracking Is Coming to VR and Beyond," CNET, February 21, 2022, https://www.cnet.com/tech/computing/watching-me-watching-you-how-eye-tracking-is-coming-to-vr-and-beyond/#:~:text=Yes%2C%20there%20are%20headsets%20that,and%20the%20Microsoft%20HoloLens%202.

188 Harrell, "Neuromarketing: What You Need to Know."

189 "Ray-Ban Stories," home page, by Ray-Ban and Meta, accessed December 14, 2022, https://www.ray-ban.com/usa/discover-ray-ban-stories/clp.

190 Alborz Geramifard, "Project CAIRaoke: Building the Assistants of the Future with Breakthroughs in Conversational AI," *Meta AI* (blog), February 23, 2022, https://ai.facebook.com/blog/project-cairaoke/.

191 Jonathan A. Obar and Anne Oeldorf-Hirsch, "The Biggest Lie on the Internet: Ignoring the Privacy Policies and Terms of Service Policies of Social Networking Services," *Information, Communication & Society* (2018): 1–20, https://papers.ssrn.com/sol3/papers.cfm?abstract_id=2757465.

192 Stefan Wojcik et al., "Bots in the Twittersphere," Pew Research Center, April 9, 2018, https://www.pewresearch.org/internet/2018/04/09/bots-in-the-twittersphere/.

193 Federal Trade Commission, "FTC Sues Owner of Online Dating Service Match.com for Using Fake Love Interest Ads to Trick Consumers into Paying for a Match.com Subscription," news release, September 25, 2019, https://www.ftc.gov/news-events/news/press-releases/2019/09/ftc-sues-owner-online-dating-service-matchcom-using-fake-love-interest-ads-trick-consumers-paying.

194 Laurel Brubaker Calkins, "Match Avoids $844 Million in FTC Claims on Judge's Ruling," *Bloomberg*, March 24, 2022, https://www.bloomberg.com/news/articles/2022-03-24/match-group-avoids-844-million-in-ftc-claims-on-judge-s-ruling.

195 Monica Anderson and JingJing Jiang, "Teens, Social Media and Technology 2018," Pew Research Center, May 31, 2018, https://www.pewresearch.org/internet/2018/05/31/teens-social-media-technology-2018/.

196 Mayo Clinic Staff, "Teens and Social Media Use: What's the Impact?" Mayo Clinic, February 26, 2022, https://www.mayoclinic.org/healthy-lifestyle/tween-and-teen-health/in-depth/teens-and-social-media-use/art-20474437.

197 *Adam Ruins Everything*, episode 26, "Adam Ruins Going Green," directed by Tim Wilkime, featuring Adam Conover, produced by Jeremy Reitz, aired December 27, 2016, on TruTV, https://www.trutv.com/shows/adam-ruins-everything.

Made in United States
Orlando, FL
02 April 2024

45381024R00161